Praise for *Not Tonight Dear, I Feel Fat*

"After decades working as a love and sex advice expert, there's no doubt there is a strong correlation between body image and sexual satisfaction. *Not Tonight Dear, I Feel Fat* is a much-needed and highly recommended book for any female who finds herself focusing on perceived body flaws to the detriment of her sex life and relationship. This book doesn't just help put a stop to negative thinking during sex; it's packed with effective, specific techniques to permanently banish body shame in the bedroom. It's a must-read for any woman who's ever worried whether her body is good enough—and isn't that most of us?"

—Tracey Cox, international bestselling author of *Hot Sex*

D1253283

NOT TONIGHT DEAR, I FEEL FAT

How to Stop Worrying About Your Body and Have Great Sex

MICHAEL ALVEAR

sourcebooks
casablanca

Published by Sourcebooks Casablanca, an imprint of Sourcebooks, Inc.
P.O. Box 4410, Naperville, Illinois 60567-4410
(630) 961-3900
Fax: (630) 961-2168
www.sourcebooks.com

Library of Congress Cataloging-in-Publication Data

Alvear, Michael.
    Not tonight dear, I feel fat : how to stop worrying about your body and have great sex
/ Michael Alvear.
        pages cm
    Includes bibliographical references.
    (pbk. : alk. paper) 1. Sex instruction for women. 2. Body image in women. 3. Women-
-Sexual behavior. 4. Sex. I. Title.
    HQ46.A544 2013
    306.7082--dc23

                                    2013001627

            Printed and bound in the United States of America.
                VP 10 9 8 7 6 5 4 3 2 1

CONTENTS

INTRODUCTION

Oh my god, he's touching it.

    Sound familiar? Just about every body-conscious woman says something like that to herself at some point during sex. The "it," of course, is the part of your body you don't like. Sometimes this is just a passing thought, but sometimes that thought gets stuck, sets up camp, and gives birth to hundreds of others like it.

You start thinking things like "I'm too fat to have sex," even though you're objectively average-sized. You tell friends you're not having sex till you're a size six. You put conditions on sex. You wear cover-up clothing. You only have sex with the lights out. You only get in positions that prevent your partner from looking at or touching certain parts of your body. Your partner starts getting a little tired of "conditional sex" and now you start having "duty sex" to avoid losing him or getting into terrible arguments. What you used to enjoy you now endure. Pretty soon your desire for any sex, conditional or not, goes away. Or your libido stays high but self-judgment paralyzes your enjoyment of making love.

Studies in academic periodicals and popular surveys show that this is an alarming trend—millions of women are losing their libido or putting off sex, even when they're in the mood—because they feel like they're too fat. Notice that last part—it's not because they *are* fat, but because they *think* they are. The problem is so bad that a study in the *Journal of Sex Research* concluded that how you feel about your body has more of an influence on sexual functioning than even menopause! Bedroom body shame is ruining sex for a growing number of women, from the petite to the plus size. They are seeing their sex lives fall off the cliff, taking their relationships along with them.

As the co-host of HBO's *Sex Inspectors*, a sex makeover series that helped couples improve their love lives, I have seen the damage that bedroom body shame can do to a relationship. In one heartbreaking episode, Sarah, who in no way, shape, or form could be considered fat, was so ashamed of her "jiggly thighs" that she would only have sex in the missionary position, and then only when the lights were out. She could only enjoy sex when her boyfriend couldn't see her body. She avoided sex more and more as a way of protecting herself, but all she managed to do was drive her boyfriend away.

Sarah had to face the fact that sexual body consciousness was threatening her relationship (and if she'd been single, it would have impinged on her ability to establish one). Diminished sexual satisfaction across time predicts the likelihood of a divorce or a breakup. Lack of sex, or the inability to enjoy it, closes you off to the kind of closeness, meaning, and connection that form the basis of relationships.

On the show I worked with all kinds of couples. Some of the women worked, some stayed at home. Some were single, some were married. Some were childless, some had children. Some were thin, some were average-sized. None were overweight but it didn't matter—they all struggled with some level of body shame in the bedroom. "*I don't deserve sex,*" one woman told me. "*Not without a flat belly.*" I can't think of anything you can say to yourself that could be so cruel. Or so wrong. Yet every night, millions of women say some version of this to themselves when their husbands and boyfriends try to express their love physically.

Women often joke that they're "having a fat day," but for too many that fat day turns into fat weeks, months, and years. What starts out as a funny phrase can turn into a not-so-funny idea: *My body isn't attractive enough for sex.* Body consciousness in the bedroom is so profound and so prevalent that sex researchers call it a "normative discontent." Meaning it's now "normal" for women to be unhappy with their bodies. This has predictably turned into rampant sexual self-consciousness—that awful feeling that some part of your body is a sexual turn-off and that if you don't fix, cover, or hide it, your partner's going to be repulsed by it.

If you're reading this book, then you're probably sexually self-conscious and looking for ways to calm your body anxiety. The uncomfortable reality is that your attempts at fixing the problem have probably made it worse. Maybe you've tried dieting and exercise with little success. Or you've avoided sex only to realize it poisons the relationship. You've put conditions on sex, but they just manage to lessen the enjoyment for everyone. You've forced yourself into "duty sex," but your partner knows you're faking it. You begin losing your libido as a subconscious effort to avoid shame-inducing sex, but now your partner feels unloved and unwanted.

All of these well-meaning but unworkable coping strategies may buy you time, but they're digging you into a deeper hole. And the first rule of holes is that when you're in one, stop digging. Admittedly, it's hard to put the shovel down and try a different approach because there doesn't seem to be one. There are no books on overcoming body anxiety to have good sex, and the few magazine articles that address the subject do a great disservice by recommending you find more creative ways of doing what you're already doing.

I've been writing about sex for twelve years. I've hosted three seasons of *Sex Inspectors.* I've answered thousands of advice-seeking emails and conducted hundreds of interviews with sex therapists, physicians, and gynecologists. And yet neither I nor any of these experts could offer a coherent path out of the problem. It wasn't just frustrating; it was heartbreaking, because so many women I care about (even in my own family) suffer from pronounced sexual self-consciousness. With twelve years of reporting on sex and access to so many credentialed experts, how could I not be able to offer a solution to the women I cared about?

So I turned to researchers who've been studying sexual self-consciousness for two decades, and it was there, deep within the stacks of academic journals, that a solution became apparent. In the last few years, scientists, therapists, researchers, and scholars have made huge advances in the understanding of how body image influences sexual functioning and satisfaction. You will find some of the research quite shocking, because it directly contradicts so many beliefs women have about themselves, the men they're attracted to, and the way they deal with their increasingly dysfunctional sex life.

For example, most women with body anxiety believe there are only three paths to restoring their sex lives: accept themselves as they are, improve their bodies through diet and exercise, or enhance their body image through positive affirmations and supportive self-talk. But studies show that these methods are difficult, impossible, or downright harmful. They can actually create *more* self-consciousness in the bedroom, not less.

If you haven't figured it out by now, significantly changing the size and shape of your body is next to impossible. And affirming a positive image of your body in the middle of an onslaught of obsessive self-hatred is like diving under an umbrella to protect you from a hurricane. Of course, the ideal solution is to accept yourself as you are, but if that were easy to do you'd already have done it.

So if improving your body or your image of it isn't the solution to sexual self-consciousness, what is? The research strongly suggests it is the very thing you've been trying so hard to avoid.

Sex.

Impossible, you say. You've had plenty of sex. How can the solution be the very thing that triggers your anxiety? Isn't that like telling a woman who's afraid of water to keep throwing herself into the deep end of the pool until she learns how to swim?

Of course not. You'd start her in ankle-deep water and help her move forward as she gets more comfortable. You'd show her how much fun it is to play in the water. You'd gossip, splash each other, and play volleyball with cute guys. You'd teach her how to get a breath whenever she needed one and how to rest in the water. You'd teach her how water supports her body and how to keep it out of her nose. You'd teach her how to float, propel, and maneuver. But mostly, you would show her *how to relax so she can be comfortable and have fun.*

It's the same with sex. All you need is a little understanding and a fair amount of direction. I'm going to show you how to have sex without paralyzing self-judgment. I'm going to show you how to manage your mind so you can stay present, attend to your pleasure, and engage with your partner. And I'm going to do it all with help from the latest peer-reviewed, academic research conducted by the most respected scientists in the field. I'll be quoting extensively from experts like Dr. Thomas F. Cash, a preeminent leader in the psychology of physical appearance, and Dr. Cindy Meston, professor of clinical psychology at the University of Texas at Austin, whose groundbreaking research is revolutionizing our understanding of exercise's impact on low libido.

This book starts by showing how your mind hijacked your body and held sex for ransom. Understanding how you got here is the first step to getting out. Then we're going to challenge a lot of assumptions you've made about men and the kinds of women they're attracted to with the latest research on male attraction. We'll move into specific approaches to raising your libido and managing your mind during sex. And finally, we'll take a look at specific sexual techniques that will help you tune in so you can get turned on.

Imagine your partner touching your belly without sending you into spasms of fear and self-hatred. Imagine having sex without a running commentary in your mind about how your body looks or what your partner thinks of it. Imagine being so involved in the pleasures of sex that you forget to "check" your thighs, or worry about your partner seeing something you're ashamed of.

This is entirely possible by changing your relationship to the problem, reframing your idea of who you are as a sexual being, understanding the principles of "crowding out" obsessive thoughts, and learning sex techniques that reduce or eliminate body shame. You deserve more than a joyless, anxiety-ridden trip through the bedroom doors. It is your destiny to have a rich, fulfilling love life.

We're just going to give fate a little nudge.

Do These Thoughts Make Me Look Fat?

Passing up Pleasure to Pass Judgment

W hen did the bedroom turn into a place to put your body on trial? When did it turn into a kangaroo court with a stacked jury and a judge banging the gavel on your looks?

Making love is your chance to experience pleasure and connect to your partner in deeper ways, not an opportunity to enter a guilty plea on charges of imperfection.

Chances are there is one thing stopping you from returning physical intimacy to its rightful place: the conviction that you shouldn't have sex until you've "improved" your body. Or, at the very least, improved your image of it.

Now it's true that having a great body or a confident image of it helps you have better sex. But the reverse is also true—having great sex improves both. Those two facts sit side by side, and like Frida Kahlo's eyebrows, they cannot be separated.

It isn't the act of sex that gives you body confidence, by the way. It's the wake it leaves behind—a deeper connection to your partner, an appreciation of what your body can do and feel, and a continued awakening of who you are, how you express yourself, and your capacity to give and receive. Those things will give you a sense of wonder, mastery, control, respect, and love that results in feeling better about your body.

But I'm getting ahead of myself. This book is not about using sex to improve your body or your self-esteem. It's about sexual insights and techniques that neutralize your self-consciousness. It's about helping you relax and enjoy making love *despite* your body anxieties and reigniting the sexual bond with your partner.

This section is the first step toward that goal. It will challenge your beliefs about sex and its relationship to physical appearance by using respected but little-known studies to refute your assumptions. In later sections, I'm going to show you how it's possible to override your obsessive thoughts through specific sexual behavior, but to make that happen, let's spend a little time on those thoughts banging around your head.

1

WHY DIETING AND EXERCISE WON'T HELP YOUR BODY IMAGE

"I've lost ten pounds and gained it back so many times I'm not sure why I even bother. Once, I lost twenty-five pounds and instead of feeling good about it I started obsessing about my cankles. It's like getting the room painted—it feels good for a couple of days until the rug starts looking bad by comparison. Then you change the rug and it feels good for a few days until the furniture starts looking scruffy. There's just no end to it."

—Cindy, 30, Fresno, California

Can diet and exercise get you closer to a body that would improve your self-image? Yes, in the same way jumping gets you closer to the sun. If it were true that losing weight improved body image, studies would show that thinner women would be more satisfied with the way their bodies look than normal-weight women. But they aren't. Studies consistently show that underweight women are nearly as dissatisfied with their bodily appearance as normal or overweight women.

From ordinary women who force themselves to eat dust for dinner to supermodels who treat cocaine as a food group, nobody is immune to distorted body perceptions. This is how bad the situation is: slender women consistently overestimate their body size more than heavier women! Supermodels have something in common with the truly overweight—they think their butts are too big.

So do professional ballet dancers. Who doesn't envy these petite flowers? If anyone knows about her body, it's a dancer who scrutinizes her physical appearance for a living. Yet one famous survey showed ballerinas significantly overestimated their true percentage of body fat!

The fact that thinner women may have an even worse body image than you do is difficult to grasp. It probably violates one of your deepest-held beliefs—that if you lost weight you'd feel better about your body. But it's true. Losing weight rarely results in an uptick in body confidence, because nearly all women are dissatisfied with their bodies.

As I mentioned in the introduction—and which I'm repeating because it's so important—researchers have come to the conclusion that body dissatisfaction is so widespread that they've labeled the phenomenon "normative discontent." In English, it means body dissatisfaction is the new normal. It is now standard and predictive that most women have a negative body image—no matter how skinny or how fat they are. It is now normal for most women to diet and try to lose weight, even if they objectively don't need to. Even if it's medically dangerous for them to try.

Of all the body image surveys done over the years, academic researchers have gravitated toward the two they consider most important: the 1997 *Shape Magazine* survey and the 1997 *Psychology Today* poll. Both support the academic contention that body satisfaction is a "normative discontent." In the *Shape* magazine survey, 90 percent of women reported feeling "somewhat, moderately, or very self-conscious about their appearance."

The *Psychology Today* survey showed that 89 percent of women wanted to lose weight. Across the board, in both surveys, women thought they were too fat. Skinny women thought they were too fat. Normal-weight women thought they were too fat. Overweight women thought they were too fat. Here are the editors of *Psychology Today*, commenting on this phenomenon:

> "The truly fat despair but there is an equivalent amount of self loathing on the part of thin people, suggesting a different type of problem (other than fat): distortion on top of dissatisfaction. Thin women distort reality by seeing themselves as fat. This type of distortion is rampant and has become the norm. 159 women in our sample are extremely underweight and 40% of them still want to lose weight.
>
> Another example that it isn't fat that's the problem: Younger women are at a weight that most women envy, but they are still plagued by feelings of inadequacy."

But I've Lost Weight Before and Felt Better...

Yes, for about ten minutes. And then you probably realized that you still didn't look like the ideal you see in the media, and a thought creeped into your self-congratulations: *If I could just lose another five pounds, THEN I'll really be satisfied.* And the struggle began anew.

Think about it—deep down, is your real goal to be thinner? Or to look like those models in the media? In the next chapter we'll talk about a "yes or no test" the media offers women. Namely, do you look like the women the media holds up as ideal? It isn't graded on a curve. You don't pass by getting closer to the ideal. You pass the test by *being* the ideal. Secretly, you know this. Ten pounds? Please. You aren't even close to passing the test. And that's why your "victory," while real, is so short-lived.

Don't get me wrong: if you are truly overweight, losing the pounds will make you feel better—you won't get out of breath as much, you'll be able to do more, move more, and prevent a lot of weight-related diseases like diabetes and heart disease. But that isn't necessarily going to improve your body image. Why?

Because the perception of your body has little to do with your actual body size.

It's simply not true that women who can fit into a size 2 dress always feel better about their bodies than women who wear a size 14. Research shows that the strongest predictor of body shame and anxiety isn't actual weight but *perceived* weight.

Dr. Michael Wiederman, in his seminal study published in the *Journal of Sex Research*, reported that 35 percent of women experience body consciousness to the point where it interfered with sex at least some of the time, but only 10 percent were objectively overweight according to the criteria set by the National Center for Health Statistics (a BMI greater than 24.9; BMI is calculated by dividing your weight [in kilograms] by the square of your height). That means over two thirds of women who experienced sex-interfering self-consciousness were normal or below normal weight!

Supermodels Have Awful Sex Lives

You might want to look like a ballerina or a supermodel, but you wouldn't want their sex lives. Studies show that models and actresses in the media have 10 to 20 percent less body fat than healthy women. They're not only in danger of the wind blowing them to the next street, but they're also more prone to sexual dysfunction than women with a healthy percentage of body fat. They're much more likely to have lower libidos and yawn-producing orgasms (not having enough body fat messes up your sexual plumbing). Yes, supermodels rule in the media, but their sex lives are locked in the castle tower. Isn't it ironic? The women you want to look like not only feel as badly about their bodies as you do, but they also actually have worse sex lives!

The average runway model is estimated to be 5 feet 9 inches tall and weigh 110 pounds—resulting in a BMI of just 16.2. A BMI of 18.5 is considered the lowest end of normal, healthy weight. Think about what that means. The media's beauty ideal is dangerous to your health. Not just bad for your self-image—*dangerous to your health*. For example, we know that women cease ovulating and menstruating when their body fat falls below about 10 percent of body weight. This is the reason for amenorrhea (absence of menstruation) in patients with anorexia nervosa and in overtrained female athletes. BMI has long established itself as a marker for health. Being outside the normal range—on either end—is a strong predictor of disease.

You Cannot See Yourself as You Are

Most women cannot accurately perceive their weight or shape. Normal-weight women consistently rate themselves as overweight, and underweight women consistently rate themselves as normal weight. It seems almost all women believe they are the reason the earth wobbles on its axis.

Researchers call it "perceived-actual disparities," or the inability to correctly perceive objective traits about your own body. This inability to see yourself as you really are is the main reason you think your partner lies when he says he loves your body. You think he sees what you do. He doesn't. His reality doesn't buy into your fiction. There's very little "perceived-actual disparity" in his assessment of you. The truth is that he's a much better judge of what your body looks like than you are.

One study that documented women's inability to judge themselves objectively found that normal-weight women who overestimated their true weight had a worse body image than normal-weight women who perceived their weight accurately. Think about this for a moment: *If you could perceive your body size accurately, your body image would improve.*

But if you're like most women, you can't. And that's why even if you lose weight, you'll most likely have a skewed perception of how you look. Weight isn't the problem. Your preoccupation with it is.

But What If I Really Am Fat?

Then you should lose weight. But not because you'll feel better about your body—because you'll feel better *period*. You should not rely on your own opinion to decide if you should lose weight. Your ability to make an informed decision is too compromised by your desire to look like those media models. Instead, use the tool preferred by most physicians—BMI.

You can check your BMI by using the National Institute for Health's automatic BMI calculator (www.nhlbisupport.com/bmi/) or a BMI chart produced by any reputable medical organization. If you find yourself outside the healthy weight category (defined as a BMI over 24.9), it's time to change your eating and exercise habits. As a rule of thumb, the average 5-foot 4-inch American woman should weigh between 108 and 144 pounds to stay within the designation of healthy weight.

Although BMI is absolutely the best way of quickly assessing healthy weight (outside of skinfold thickness measurements with calipers and other procedures that require a doctor's supervision), it has a few quirks you should be aware of. Because it does not distinguish between bones, muscle, fat, or organs, BMI can and often does mislabel some people as overweight when they are not. Muscle weighs more than fat, so BMI can be problematic for athletic women.

BMI can also sometimes label you as normal weight when a caliper exam shows you're overweight. Despite these problems BMI is fairly accurate for the vast majority of people. If you sense that your BMI index isn't accurate, make an appointment with your doctor so he can do a custom body fat check and determine your weight classification.

> "I only get in sexual positions that prevent my partner from looking at or touching parts of my body I'm ashamed of."

Despite research to the contrary, it's hard to let go of the idea that losing weight will make you happier about your body. After all, you were taught that thinness is the secret to happiness from the time you were a little girl. Somehow, some way, you have to make peace with the startling reality uncovered by twenty years of academic research:

Being thinner does not make women happier.

The Least Effective Way of Improving Your Sex Life

Since body image is such a strong predictor of sexual functioning and satisfaction, the answer to improving your sex life seems obvious: improve your body or your image of it. We've just seen that "improving" your body through diet and exercise cannonballs you to a net that catapults you right back to where you started. Is working on your body image more effective? Will reciting positive affirmations in front of the mirror, correcting self-talk, and keeping body image diaries help? Yes, but only in the way that sofa change helps pay the rent.

It's not that trying to improve your body image is a bad thing; it's just that it has some excruciating obstacles. How on earth are you going to look in the mirror and convince yourself that you have a beautiful body? You may in fact have one, but as you just saw, women are very poor judges of what their body looks like. To most women, "positive thinking" their way into feeling better about their body amounts to lying and self-delusion.

While it may seem obvious to attack the problem directly, the shortest distance between two points is rarely a straight line. You might only be five hundred yards from the top of the mountain, but unless you've got the gear—and the stomach—to climb up its sheer wall, you'd be much safer (and get there faster) using the switchbacks.

There are two reasons that the direct method—"working on your body image"—is at best insufficient and at worst ineffective. First, it keeps the focus on your body and how it looks when you should be concentrating on things that have nothing to do with your appearance. Second, focusing on your looks runs the risk of actually perpetuating the sexual dysfunction you're trying to resolve. See, right now, you've probably made the decision that you won't have sex (at least not without a lot of conditions and concealments) until you lose ten pounds or feel better about your- self (whichever comes first). I call it the if/then "sex diet." It goes something like this: If you lose weight, then you'll make love. If you feel better about your body, then you'll have sex. Well, diets never work and this one won't either. Sex is not the reward for losing weight. It's the reward for being human.

This sex diet, or self-imposed sexual "time-out," which is extremely common among women with low body esteem, actu- ally reinforces the idea that you don't deserve sex unless you look a certain way. You're actually punishing yourself for the way you look. What a terrible line of thinking!

Since when do you have to *earn* the right to love or be loved? Since when is weight love's wages? Conditional love has no place in our lives. You are lovable *because*. Period. Not *because* you are, or will soon be, thin. Not *because* fill-in-the-blank. Just *because*.

Sex is not a reward for becoming; it's the reward for being.

2

HOW YOU ENDED UP HOLDING SEX FOR RANSOM

"The first guy I ever slept with told me I was fat. We were in college, and looking back, I know now that I wasn't. I just wasn't super-skinny. But ever since then, I have felt really self-conscious in bed. Even today, I just can't seem to let go and enjoy myself because I'm worried my body isn't 'good enough' for my boyfriend. But here's the funny thing: I know I'm attractive and that my boyfriend is crazy about me. Yet I keep having the same thoughts: 'My thighs are too big, my stomach is pooching out too much.' Even when he's making passionate love to me, I can't help thinking that he's fantasizing about someone thinner. I'd never admit it to him, but sometimes I have stronger orgasms when I'm by myself—because I'm not worried about how I look..."
—Sandra, 28, Toledo, Ohio

There are three aspects to body image: judgment (the level of satisfaction or dissatisfaction with your physical attributes), the emotional impact of your judgment, and the "investment" you make—the level of self-worth you draw from your appearance and the lengths you'll go to enhance or manage it.

Keep this definition in mind as we go forward: judgment, impact, and investment. It will help you understand the influence your body image has in the bedroom.

The Culprit behind a Bad Self-Image

There are many factors that contribute to a negative body image—growing up in a judgmental family that stressed dieting, children who made disparaging comments about the way you look, a competitive girl culture that thrives on judgment, encourages rivalries, and magnifies the importance of appearances, and of course, being objectively overweight or obese. But there's a bigger reason for your body self-consciousness—a much bigger reason: the extent to which you buy into, compare yourself to, and try to achieve the media's ideal of feminine beauty. There is no other factor that comes close.

> "I don't deserve the pleasure of sex because my thighs are too big."

The main reason most women have such a poor self-image is because not only have they accepted the media's beauty ideal, but they also have invested heavily in trying to achieve its anatomically impossible standards. This is not some feminist polemic espoused by scholars with a political agenda. *It is the conclusion of nearly every academic study ever done on the issue of body image.* Let me explain how researchers discovered this.

It started with academic research on eating disorders. Researchers suspected that eating-disordered women were somehow affected by the relentless, ubiquitous, inescapable images of below-normal-weight women on TV, magazines, movies, and the Internet. After years of research, a clear picture emerged: the media's presentation of a single standard of below-healthy-weight beauty and the compulsion toward conformity it generated was the main cause in the development of eating disorders like anorexia nervosa and bulimia. The relationship was simple, clear, and replicated across nearly every study ever done: the more you internalize the media's below-normal-weight ideal, the more you invest in trying to conform to it, the more likely you will develop a diagnosable eating disorder.

That all might be interesting, but if you're like most women, you don't have an eating disorder. What does this have to do with you and the problems you face in the bedroom?

In the past ten years, body image research has focused more on "healthy" women, or rather women who do not have diagnosable eating disorders. The thinking went something like this: If the media's relentless presentation of a single standard of beauty is a leading cause of eating disorders, what else might it be a leading cause of?

So, researchers got to work on it. The next wave of body image research, conducted by experts like Dr. Michael Wiederman, Professor of Psychology at Columbia College, specifically excluded eating-disordered women.

As stated before, there are several contributing causes to body shame—your family, the judgments of both men and women, how much you compete with other women, and how objectively overweight you are. But researchers found that the strongest predictor of body dissatisfaction in healthy women is the same as it is for eating-disordered women—the extent to which you internalize the media's standard for thinness. The more you agree with the below-healthy thin ideal, the more you compare

> "I have turned down sex even though I was in the mood because I felt ashamed of my body."

yourself against it, the more you invest in trying to achieve that standard, the more dissatisfied you will be with your body.

Let me give you a small example of just how insidious the media's standard of beauty is in affecting your self-esteem. Dr. Laura Choate of Louisiana State University published a fascinating study in the *Journal of Counseling & Development*. She had a group of women read news magazines while another group read fashion magazines. There were no differences between the groups in age, height, or weight. Yet when they filled out a body image assessment immediately after reading the magazines, an amazing picture emerged: The women who read the fashion magazines reported greater body dissatisfaction and a lower ideal body weight than women who read the news magazines. *They were only reading the magazines for fifteen minutes.* As Dr. Choate's study concluded, "Even brief exposure to media images portraying the sociocultural ideal directly shapes perceptions of the ideal body type expected for women."

It would be one thing if there were just a few studies showing the media's corrosive impact on women's self-esteem, but I couldn't find a single study published in the last twenty years that didn't come to the same conclusion. For example, one study exposed a group of women to ads with thin models while the other group exposed women to the same product ads without any models. The women who viewed ads with models rated their body satisfaction lower than the women who viewed the product ads without the models.

Supermodels Create Appearance Anxiety in Men, Too

It's well documented that when women see impossibly beautiful women in magazines, their body image drops faster than Marie Antoinette's guillotine. But the most fascinating studies show that men report significant body consciousness when exposed to gorgeous women in magazines, too. For example, in a study published in *Human Communication Research* (2009), Dr. Jennifer Aubrey at the University of Missouri found that men exposed to ads and editorial features with beautiful women suffered immediate and long-lasting body consciousness. This confounded Dr. Aubrey because the men were mainly exposed to images of women. Why would men have such a dramatic reaction to images of beautiful women? In a later study, Dr.

Aubrey answered her own question: The supermodels reminded men that they weren't good-looking enough to date such beautiful women! In yet another study, this time in the **North American Journal of Psychology** (2006), male subjects were exposed to photographs of muscular men in magazines like **Maxim, FHM,** and **Men's Health.** Immediately after exposure they reported significantly lower levels of body satisfaction.

If that ain't poetic justice, I don't know what is.

The media's power to make you feel bad about how you look is almost omnipotent. Once you submerge yourself in over two decades of body image research, it's easy to reach a startling conclusion: reading a fashion magazine does to your body image what smoking does to your lungs.

But Isn't the Media Just Reflecting What Guys Want?

Everybody knows that men want the kind of skinny chicks the media presents. Everybody, that is, except guys. It's news to them. As you'll see later in the book, attractiveness studies show that men seldom pick the below–healthy-weight body types you see in the media as their ideal form of beauty.

This is a critical point to absorb because so much of your suffering is based on a demonstrably false assumption of what guys like. Yes, men judge women harshly. Yes, they base their desire almost entirely on appearances (at least at first). In fact, they emphasize it so much they're unwilling to have any type of romantic relationship unless they are first sexually attracted. The Male Gaze is alive and well, but what it seeks is not the unhealthy women you see on TV, magazines, and movies. Men are turned on by what you rarely see in the media: normal curves, healthy weight, and slender-to-average waist-to-hip ratios. It isn't men insisting that you be so skinny to be desirable—it's you. You internalized the media's beauty ideal and projected it onto what men want.

Let's look at one of the most fascinating body image studies done in the last ten years. Researchers at UCLA wanted to know which contributed more to women's body dissatisfaction: the ubiquitous media standard of beauty or the desire for male attention.

Well, the only way to separate those variables is to study women who are not interested in men—lesbians. So they designed a study ("Body Image Satisfaction In Heterosexual, Gay, And Lesbian Adults," *Archives Of Sexual Behavior*, 2009) that recruited gay women to participate in the same kind of study typically reserved for heterosexual women. The researchers were convinced that lesbians would have much higher body esteem because they are not motivated by the reward of male attention. If they didn't want, welcome, or seek male attention, it made sense that they'd score higher on body esteem assessments.

Well, a funny thing happened on the way to proving that hypothesis. It was completely wrong. Lesbians were not at a lower risk for body dissatisfaction than heterosexual women. As the researchers concluded, "It is widely assumed that the desire to attract and retain a male partner contributes to body image concerns. The finding that lesbians (who desire female partners) and heterosexual women (who seek male partners) are similar in body dissatisfaction raises questions about the relative importance of attracting a mate versus adhering to broader cultural ideals of attractiveness for women's body satisfaction."

This is an astounding conclusion: The media has more power to influence your body image than the men you're trying to attract.

How the Media Gets You to Hate Your Body

So, an older fish swims up to two younger fish and she says, "Hi, girls, how's the water?" The young fish smile, nod, and the older fish swims away. About a minute later, one of the young fish turns to the other and says, "What the hell is water?"

To understand the process of how media gets you to hate your body, you first have to realize, like the older fish in the story, that you're surrounded by water—in the form of endlessly repeating images of a single form of feminine beauty; an inescapable, singularly monolithic idea of what you're supposed to look like if you want male attention and female admiration. Once you realize the "water" you're swimming in, it's easier to understand the reaction so many women have to the image overload: *There must be something wrong with me because I don't look like that.*

Your conviction that there is something seriously wrong with your body—that it needs work, that it is not worthy of looking at and especially not worthy of having sex—is not a fact you discovered; it's a fiction thrust upon you. You didn't make the judgment that there's something wrong with the way you look. The media did. You just bought into it. You did not come to the conclusion that you should be ashamed of your body. The media did. You merely accepted it.

But how is that possible? The images of thinner-than-healthy women may be inescapable, but they're just images. Even if they're repeated endlessly, how can they make you feel so bad about yourself? Because the singular representation of beauty isn't just presented as an ideal but as the solution to all your problems, the path to a happy life, the road to sexual ecstasy. If you look like the women they present, you'll get your man. If you can fit into a size two, you'll get the respect you crave. If you can take the curves out of your figure, you'll put love into your life. If you can get your thighs to look like tubes, you'll be the envy of all women. If you could just look like the media-sponsored women, men would fight over you, shower you with attention, and make you feel loved and cared for. If you just looked like them, sex would be something you'd deserve, look forward to, be confident about, and get pleasure from.

The media purposefully presents these skinnier-than-possible models because they're trying to move product. They can't sell diet books, plans, and programs to women who are satisfied with their bodies. They can't sell slimming foods or exercise regimens to women who like their form and shape. They can't sell magazines filled with beauty makeovers to women who think they look fine. No need means no sale. Therefore, they must create a need, and the best way to do that is to create dissatisfaction. Advertisers are quite literally giving you a problem so they can sell a solution. From *Cosmopolitan* magazine ("Get a Banging Beach Bod in Three Days!") to *People* magazine ("Fastest Celebrity Post-Baby Slim-Downs") to *O, The Oprah Magazine* ("Dress 10 Pounds Slimmer"), the messages are clear and unmistakable: there's a problem with the way you look, and we know how to solve it.

Media to Women: Get Thin or Get Out

The media's feminine ideal comes with a premise (thinness is vital to personal happiness) and a promise (thinness solves every problem, especially in bed). The playbook is clear: get thin or get out. You either get as thin as those models or you're doomed to a lonely life without male attention or female admiration.

Now, who wants to be damned into eternal loneliness? Who wants to be invisible to men? Disrespected by women? Celibate in the bedroom? Understandably, you don't want to be left behind. You see how everybody is constantly observing and evaluating the female form and you understand, intuitively, that you must also. In order to be loved and accepted, you must be able to present your body the way the media presents bodies. You must be able to look at and evaluate your body the same way others do or you won't know if you're acceptable. So, you do what a lot of women in your situation do. You…

Take On the Role of Observer

Slowly, gradually, without knowing it, from the time you were a little girl, you agreed to take on the role of observer of your own body. Just like so many look at you as something to be evaluated, as an object that might be worthy of desire, you slowly started observing and evaluating your body the way others do. And now you devote a great deal of your attention to self-surveillance, habitually and constantly monitoring your body's outward appearance.

But what happens when you observe that your body doesn't look like the media ideal? You react the same way you react to any public rejection, like being benched in front of your teammates, being passed over for promotion, or failing a college entrance or medical board. You react with shame, guilt, worthlessness, anger, and self-loathing. You call yourself stupid, lazy, incapable of discipline. You get anxious that others will see your obvious failure and judge you. You become afraid of being the butt of jokes. They'll say you're so dumb you got locked in a grocery store and died of starvation. They'll say your blood type is Ragu. And if they don't make the insults, you'll gladly do it for them.

Every day, the media asks you to take a "yes or no" test: *Do you look like the women we say are beautiful?* Pass the test and you get rich, handsome men to adore you over a candlelit dinner. Fail it and you spend Saturday night alone eating cat food.

If you buy into this fiction—caviar if you pass the media's beauty test, cat food if you don't—you are destined to a world of hurt. It is anatomically impossible for all but the tiniest fraction of women to look like the ideal of beauty the media peddles. For example, the average fashion model has a BMI of 17.1, according to Will Lassek, MD, a former assistant surgeon general, while the average American woman has a BMI of 28.1. Unless you're already there or close to it, trying for it is a recipe for self-hatred. You'll look at your shortcomings and have a field day with the disappointments.

You'll dislike yourself, sure, but the real hatred will be reserved for the uncooperating body parts—the tummy that won't go flat no matter how many crunches you do, the thighs that won't slim down no matter how much you run.

But you persevere anyway. You formulate an action plan. You start investing a lot into your appearance, particularly dieting and exercise. You blast your butt, feel the burn, crunch those abs. You mainline hope into your veins. You don't buy that bullshit about the anatomical impossibility of achieving the kind of body you see flickering on the screen or staring out at you from every magazine page. Yes, you're average size for an American woman—close to 5 feet 4 inches and 142 pounds. And yes, those media beauties are 5 feet 9 inches and 110 pounds. But it can be done. You're sure of it. Maybe you can't grow five inches, but you can lose thirty pounds, drop four dress sizes, and decrease your body mass index by a third *if you just worked hard enough.* How do you know? Because the media tells you so. Why are they telling you? Because they've got product to move. So they create the need, then the hope, and finally, the sale.

> "I avoid certain sexual positions because I'm afraid of how my partner will react when he sees parts of my body I'm ashamed of."

Every day they trot out new workouts and diets that promise eternal salvation from the mirror. They treat the body as a construction site, assuring you that with the right motivation and materials you can turn stadiums into skyscrapers.

So you go for it. Again and again. And fail again and again. Oh sure, you have moments, true victories, but they're temporary. The only thing you end up losing permanently is balance and self-respect. The cycle of self-loathing is set: Try, fail, shame. Try, fail, guilt. Try, fail, despair. You live out a daily pattern: compare your body to the media ideal, constantly monitor it for flaws, spend time and money trying to fix it, then collapse into a cycle of shame, depression, and despair.

But enough about the first half of your day. Let's move on.

How This Plays Out in the Bedroom

Now that we know how you got in this mess, let's answer a specific question: Exactly how does a poor body image affect you in the bedroom? Studies have shown body image has a direct cause-and-effect relationship with almost all sexual functioning. A poor body image can choke the life out of your libido. It can make you turn down sex even when you want it. It distracts your attention from pleasurable physical feelings to your perceived imperfections. The shame lowers or eliminates your ability to ask for the things that turn you on, reducing the overall pleasure of an experience. It forces you to emotionally disengage from what's going on, leading to difficulty climaxing or less pleasurable orgasms. As stated before, a study in the *Journal of Sex Research* went as far as saying that body image has as much of an impact on sexuality as menopause.

Let's concentrate on desire for a moment, as low libido is one of the issues that women complain about most. Body anxieties can turn you into a sexual camel—somebody who can go great lengths of time without sex. A simple study was conducted a few years back that powerfully demonstrated the link between body esteem and libido. Women were asked to read aloud an erotic story and then asked about the state of their sexual desire. Women with a negative body image reported much lower arousal levels than women with positive self-judgments.

> "I want to want to have sex, but at least my lack of desire keeps me from experiencing shame and embarrassment."

The link between body image and sexual desire does not correlate with actual body size, by the way. Studies are remarkably consistent in their conclusion that BMI (body mass index—the

> "I refuse to have sex unless I wear lingerie or clothing that covers up my flaws."

ratio of height to weight) is not related to levels of sexual desire. In other words, your weight isn't the problem; it's your *perception* of your weight. To be clear, actually being overweight or obese increases susceptibility to a poor body image, but studies show that body image is far more important than actual body mass in predicting sexual function.

Which brings me to a refrain you're going to hear often: Unless you are seriously overweight, losing weight is not going to improve your sex life. Let me repeat this. If you are waiting to have sex until you lose ten pounds, forget it. It's the *perception* of your body, rather than your *actual* body size, that's affecting your experience of sex.

Researchers have known for years that body image has a profound impact on women's sexual functioning. They've examined the effects, documented them, and then replicated the results with a multitude of studies over the last twenty years. They know what it does, but it's only recently that they've been able to explain *how* it does it. While there are differing variations among academics, the critical path pretty much goes like this:

Self-objectification
You take on the role of the observer.

Self-surveillance
You scrutinize, inspect, and monitor your physical attributes for perceived imperfections.

Appearance anxiety

The self-surveillance reveals that you are not, in fact, a super-model. So you invest a lot of time, money, and energy trying to upgrade your appearance to acceptable standards, but the self-judgments don't go away. Your fear of being evaluated, scorned, and rejected results in a constant preoccupation with weight and other aspects of your appearance. You're caught in a cycle of shame, embarrassment, and anxiety.

Self-consciousness in the bedroom

Appearance anxiety compels you to avoid sexual positions that give your partner an unflattering view of your body. You insist on lights out, and wear some type of camouflage clothing. You feel inhibited, passive, and unable to articulate preferences that would make sex more enjoyable. You restrict your movements in bed to ensure limited views of your body.

Unwanted sexual problems

You experience a significant reduction or a complete loss of desire. You emotionally disengage from your partner. You experience reduced physical sensations because your attention is focused on your appearance. You find it difficult to climax, and when you can, it is less pleasurable than it used to be.

This is the typical way self-conscious women experience sex, and it is no wonder that they seek relief in any way they can. But the preferred solutions (lights out, covering up) aggravate the problem. You don't need to get a better body or improve your image of it to experience wonderful, shame-free sex. You can do it by activating a series of feedback loops that I'm about to introduce.

3

THE SURPRISING SOLUTION TO SELF-CONSCIOUSNESS

"Spanx won't prevent his hands from touching what I'm trying to cover up, but I use it anyway. I feel like I lessen the damage if I keep him from seeing what he wants to touch."
—Sophia, 28, Grand Rapids, Michigan

Let me be bold and say that sex is not the problem. The way you're having it is. Before you throw this book on the floor, hear me out. Often, this is what happens: in your attempt to alleviate your sexual anxiety, you came up with short-term fixes (avoidance, covering up, restricting positions, emotionally disengaging, dieting, exercise) that perpetuated the problem and sucked you into an unresolvable vicious cycle. These solutions require you to pay *more* attention to your appearance ("Have I covered enough of my belly?" "Is it dark enough that he can't see my thighs?" "Have I exercised enough to shape my butt?"). Your solutions end up magnifying the appearance anxiety and heightening the significance of the problem.

Instead of looking at the nature of the solution, you looked at the quality of your effort and doubled down on your attempts. You read magazine articles that encouraged you to keep doing what you're doing only with new, creative avoidance behaviors.

This not only made the problem worse, but it also in many ways *became* the problem. Now, every session becomes an opportunity to practice the problem. Pretty soon the dogged repetition of behavior that doesn't work leaves you frustrated, hopeless. Now you're struggling with the problem *and* the attempt to solve it. Sex changed from an act of lovemaking to an act of problem-solving. You're tumbling in a vicious cycle where one trouble leads to another that aggravates the first.

Let's Change Your Approach to Sex

There is a way of having sex that reduces or eliminates appearance anxiety. There are sexual techniques that can suspend self-judgment, lower obsession, and raise self-confidence. You don't have to shut off the lights, cover up, diet, or exercise to fight your anxiety. You just have to learn a new way of having sex.

This, of course, is problematic. If you're too self-conscious to have sex, if you do everything you can to postpone or put conditions on it, how in God's pajamas are you ever going to have it without the paralyzing effects of your self-judgments?

That will become clear as we move forward. First, let's take a look at *why* the research points to sex as the solution to self-consciousness. Scientists and scholars who study body image and the impact it has on women's sexuality have made some counter-intuitive discoveries. For example:

Sex Improves Body Image

Researchers have known for years that body image is a critical component of the sexual experience. But they've also observed the reverse—how sexual experiences influence body image. This led to chicken-or-the-egg debates: Does a positive body image create satisfying sex, or does satisfying sex create a positive body image? Most researchers believe there's a dual feedback loop at work: Great sexual experiences *form* positive body images, which in turn creates satisfying sex, which then strengthens your body image.

The relationship between body image and sexual experience is reciprocal. Your thoughts shape your experiences and your experiences shape your thoughts. It's not just academics who observe this dynamic; it's borne out by the opinion of a great many women. In a *Psychology Today* survey of 4,500 women, 67 percent felt that good sexual experiences contribute to satisfactory feelings about their bodies.

Researchers often make "accidental" discoveries. Sometimes they search for silver and end up with gold. One of their 24-carat revelations has to do with the impact of sexual skills. Namely that...

Sexual Competence Gives You Bedroom Confidence

Being good in bed reduces appearance anxiety. Women who consider themselves "good in bed" have the highest levels of positive body image. This discovery has important implications for solving self-consciousness. Improving your sexual skills will do far more for your self-image than simply staring at a mirror, reciting positive affirmations, and trying to convince yourself that you look beautiful.

The Great Sexual Paradox

Allow me to introduce a great paradox researchers have wrestled with for years: Positive body image has *enormous* influence on satisfying sex, but satisfying sex doesn't require a positive body image.

The contradiction became apparent by the undeniably high number of test subjects that score high on both body *dissatisfaction* and sexual *satisfaction*. How could this be possible in the face of all the evidence that a positive body image is crucial to good sex? Researchers must have gotten that confused look ostriches get when they hear a whistle. But as they investigated this surprising phenomenon, they found a few qualities of intimacy that explained the contradiction.

Sex Drains the Charge out of Negative Body Images

Sex "habituates" body consciousness. Habituation means you get so used to a stimulus that it can't elicit the same response. For example, when you first enter a room, you might get distracted by the noisy sound from the old air-conditioning unit. But over time, you ignore the sound, even though it's still present.

With enough satisfying sexual experiences, women habituate to their low body esteem. Sex no longer elicits anxiety or self-consciousness even though their negative body image remains intact. Like the sound of the air-conditioning unit, they cannot hear the racket of their appearance anxiety, even though it's still there.

Researchers also noted a phenomenon closely related to habituation: You can have negative judgments about your body without dwelling on it or punishing yourself for it. It's possible to think that the slight jiggle in your thighs is a slap-on-the-wrist misdemeanor rather than a felony that gets you ten to twenty in the big house. It's possible to believe that sex would be better with a flat tummy and *still have great sex*.

In other words, beliefs about your body don't have to get in the way of your pleasure. How many times have you gotten ready for a night on the town, looked in the mirror, didn't like what you saw, went out, and had a blast anyway? You don't need to like how you look to have a good time, in or out of bed. This is an important concept to grasp: liking how you look is preferable, but not necessary, to enjoying sex.

You can hate your backhand and still enjoy tennis. You are not always incapacitated by the fact that you don't like something about yourself. This is an important principle to remember as we begin restoring your sex life, but not as important as understanding that…

A Strong Sense of Well-Being Is More Powerful Than Body Image

Well-being is defined as the quality of our mental, physical, and emotional lives when we account for health, happiness, attainment of pleasure, avoidance of pain, relationships, meaning, and self-realization. Obviously, sex is a crucial component to an overall sense of well-being. It is an integral part of the communication, respect, companionship, and relationship satisfaction that gives you a higher quality of life.

Researchers have recently concluded that a strong sense of well-being is more important than body image in predicting sexual functioning. They base this belief on a simple observation: Women who score high on well-being but low on body image report greater sexual satisfaction than women who score low on well-being but high on body image. In other words, improving other parts of your life will do more for your love life than improving your body image.

From Vicious Cycle to Virtuous Circle

Let's review these discoveries: Positive sex experiences produce positive body images. Having regular, satisfying sex can override, reduce, or eliminate body anxiety. Being good at sex builds body confidence. Satisfying sex habituates self-consciousness. Sex contributes greatly to an overall sense of well-being, which exerts a greater influence on sexual functioning than body image. At this point, the answer to your body image woes should be obvious:

Sex is the solution to self-consciousness.

If you look at the research discoveries closely, you'll notice a series of feedback loops:

1. Body image affects sex. Sex affects body image.
2. Good sex contributes to an overall sense of well-being, and overall well-being produces good sex.
3. Competence breeds confidence, which grows competence. The better you get at sex, the better you feel about your body. The better you feel about your body, the better you'll get at sex.

Our goal is to take you out of the vicious cycle you're in to the virtuous circle I just described. In a vicious cycle one trouble leads to another that aggravates the first. In a virtuous circle one accomplishment leads to another that encourages the first. Both operate on a feedback loop—the results of the output feed back to the input.

You may be wondering how you can put yourself into a virtuous circle if sex has become such a source of shame that you avoid, postpone, or put conditions on it. How are you supposed to have sex when you dread it? The short answer is that I'm going to show you ways of having sex that reduce and eventually eliminate the stress you experience, but for now, there's one thing we need to clear up. And that's this silly idea you have about what type of bodies turn men on.

4

WHAT SCIENTIFIC STUDIES REVEAL ABOUT THE BODIES MEN PREFER

"I'll be having a great time watching TV with my boyfriend when a beautiful model in a commercial comes on and I just lose it. I go from thinking 'He's in love with me' to 'He's settling for me.' Same thing when he gets those 'babe of the day' pics on his gaming sites. I know he's comparing me to them and thinking, 'I wish she'd look like that.' It's not like he says it or acts that way, but he doesn't have to. Guys say they don't necessarily want a skinny girl with big boobs, but they always snap to attention when one of them walks by."
—Alicia, 24, Atlanta, Georgia

W hat do men want in a woman? What do they want women to look like? It's important to know because you'll have a much better chance of attracting male attention if you know what makes men say "hubba hubba." This is simple evolutionary mate selection at work, and it applies to males as well. They have little chance of attracting females if they don't know what females are attracted to.

You'd think that women would be experts at knowing how men want them to look, but the research proves otherwise. Women so consistently overestimate male preferences for slenderness that it leaves some researchers wondering what world women are living in.

Let's take a quick look at how academics discovered the discrepancy between what men like and what women *think* men like. In the typical study, men and women are presented with representations of the female form—from very thin to very fat (these figures are mostly line drawings, but some studies use silhouettes, illustrations, or photographs). They are then asked to circle shapes that represent:

1. Their ideal body shape
2. What they believe members of the opposite sex prefer

The results? Women overestimate male preferences for slenderness. Constantly. Consistently. In nearly every study. This phenomenon baffles researchers because it's completely at odds with the prevailing theory of how men and women pair up.

Mate selection theory holds that women intuitively know what men prefer; otherwise, they wouldn't know how to attract them. This ability also allows them to assess their "relative value" compared to women they're competing against. This is an evolutionary characteristic that facilitates procreation in all species. Knowing male preferences allows females to feature the characteristics that will attract them.

Why are women losing their ability to gauge male preferences? Researchers theorize it's a direct result of the media's relentless presentation of women who can fit between a door and its frame. As the authors of a 1995 study in *Sex Roles* noted:

"The media images emphasizing thinness cause a woman to downscale her own ideal size from her real size rating but may be powerful enough to cause her to distort her perception of her partner's ideal female."

The authors of a study published in *Journal of American Psychology* on sex differences in perceptions of desirable body shape were particularly blunt in their assessment: "Our data suggest that women are misinformed and exaggerate the magnitude of thinness that men desire," write the authors, "probably as a result of promotion of thinness in women through advertising by the diet industry."

Women are just as bad at estimating what kind of bust lines men prefer. Breast size preference studies (yes, they exist—don't ask me how they got their funding) show that females believe men like larger breasts than men actually report.

What Men Actually Prefer

Okay, so now we know what women *think* men like, and it's wrong. What's right? What body types do men prefer? The only way to find out is to ask them, and that's what a great many researchers have done. Before I share the results, let's talk about how these studies were conducted.

When studying male preferences, researchers use two essential measurements of female attractiveness. The first is waist-to-hip ratio (WHR), which you get by dividing the circumference of your waist by the circumference of your hips.

A narrow waist set against full hips has been a consistent feature of female attractiveness throughout most of history. Because it's such an erotic marker, women have put themselves through a lot of pain to achieve the look. The earliest cosmetic surgery in England consisted of removing two lower ribs to enhance the narrowness of the waist. It also explains the popularity of corsets, despite the internal injuries it caused so many women. The corset was replaced by girdles, then by wide belts, and today, Spanx.

The second measure of attractiveness researchers use is the body mass index (BMI). Interestingly, BMI is a far greater predictor of attractiveness than WHR. But whether it's measured by WHR or BMI, studies consistently find that men are attracted to women who fall between the low to middle range *of the normal scale*. Let me repeat those last four words: of the normal scale. Not the media's version of normal, but life's version of normal. Because this is going to come as a shock to many women, I want to repeat the conclusive findings:

Men are most attracted to normal-weight women.

Yes, they prefer "slender" body types, but within healthy, normal weight. They don't like throwing bread to a woman and having it come back sliced. *They are not attracted to the ideal of beauty presented by most media.* They are attracted to healthy-looking women.

I want you to understand why men will never be attracted to the level of thinness you're so invested in. From an evolutionary standpoint, men are drawn to women who show strong signs of fertility. Because there are no physical signs of a woman's capacity to bear and nurse children, men use an indirect marker—beauty. But for beauty to be a reliable marker of fertility, it must have characteristics linked to health.

This is why WHR and BMI are such accurate predictors of men's preferences—because they correlate strongly with health and fecundity. For example, it's been proven that a lower WHR (within the normal range) is an accurate indicator of reproductive potential and long-term health risk.

Men look for clues to fertility by the way you look. And what are those clues? A WHR and a BMI in the low-to-midpoint of *normal*. Again, not the media's definition of normal. Life's definition of normal.

Now, get what I'm saying here. *Nature did not give men a choice.* They always have and always will be attracted to women who show strong signs of fertility. Yes, men are attracted to a wide variety of "types" (height, hair color, bust lines, etc.), but their attraction will always be guided by a woman's potential for reproductive success. And health is the only outward sign of it.

Given these facts, it stands to reason that men are not attracted to women so thin you can blindfold them with dental floss. In one particularly interesting study in the *Journal of Personality and Social Psychology*, researchers tested male preferences between the media's ideal of tubular shapes against hourglass figures that are so representative of fertility. It wasn't even close. Men strongly preferred women with hourglass shapes over tubular shapes.

But Those Men Online Say They Want Thin Women

So guys on dating sites say in their profiles that they want to date thin women. Isn't that proof that men like thin women? Yes, but the male version of thin and your version of it are two different things. You can get an interesting peek into the male calculation of thinness by looking at a particularly clever study from the University Of New Mexico. It sought out men who explicitly stated they wanted "thin" women in personal ads. When these men were presented with line-drawn figures, they circled *several* figures they found attractive, not just the thin figures.

In other words, even when the men stated a "thin" preference, they were actually attracted to a wide range of body sizes. The most interesting finding: 73 percent of males indicated they would *not* want to date a woman comparable to the thinnest figure in the line drawings (the ones that most approximate the media ideal).

So why did the men who explicitly stated they were looking for "thin" women in their profiles rate female figures "attractive" up to the midpoint of the weight range scale? Researchers believe they weren't discriminating against women in the normal weight range as much as they were trying to discourage overweight women from contacting them.

Men vs. Media

At the end of the day, you have to decide what you value most: men's preferences or the media's presentations. They are two very different things. And yet it seems that women have cast their lot with the media. They keep betting on the wrong horse and wonder why they're broke.

Unlike the media ideal, men are not attracted to women who are thin in an unhealthy way. Unlike the media ideal, men are attracted to women who fall between the low-to-midpoint range of normal BMI and WHR. Unlike the media, men have a far wider range of body shapes they find attractive.

The choice is yours. Do you want to appeal to men or the media? Might I suggest that if you're going to let other people define beauty for you, at least let it be the men you're attracted to, not magazine editors you've never met.

But What about My Guy?

Now that we know what men as a species are attracted to, let's talk about a very specific male—the one you're dating, hooking up with, or sharing a life with.

Is he lying when he says your body turns him on?

If you're like most body-conscious women, you probably don't believe your partner when he says you have a beautiful body. You convict him of sexual perjury—lying to get laid.

You won't get an argument from me—men lie for sex. We practically carry business cards that say "Professional Liar." But once again, there's a flaw in your logic. Yes, men will say anything to get laid. *To a woman he finds attractive.* Men don't lie to women they find unattractive.

See, you have to understand something about men. We give our penises nicknames so we can be on a first-name basis with the person making all of our decisions. And while we lie to do Mr. Happy's bidding, Mr. Happy himself is incapable of lying.

You can't argue with a hard penis

It's really difficult for a man to get an erection for a woman he's not attracted to. If he's trying to get you in bed, it's because your body turns him on. Viagra, Levitra, and Cialis prove my point. They don't work unless a man is turned on. Viagra and its cousins affect the plumbing, not the desire. They can open up the valves to let more blood into the penis, but they cannot make a man want you. You may be resentful at times of the penis's persistence or its alarming lack of conscience, but never, ever doubt its sincerity.

The belief that your guy wants "it" and not you understandably makes you upset. But that's only because you think men subscribe to a three-word sexual philosophy: Anything That Moves. It hurts him to be accused of wanting to get off without wanting you. It's true that he wants "it." It's also true that he wants "it" to be you.

He thinks you're beautiful

The media doesn't portray normal-weight or overweight women very often. No matter where you look, there you aren't. So when your guy tells you how beautiful you look, how much you turn him on, you think he's lying to spare your feelings. After all, how can he look up from a magazine with a picture of the latest supermodel and honestly say he finds you beautiful?

The same way you can look up from the cover of a romance novel and say it to him.

See, there's a design flaw in your conviction. That model on the cover of a magazine may inspire lust, but it's a one-dimensional lust. It's a fake image, not a real woman. And because it's an image, it only operates on the visual level. Now, I don't want to diminish how important the visual is to guys (where would the porn industry be without it?), but the formula to desire is a far more complex equation. The way you smell, the way you feel, how you taste, the timbre of your voice—*all* of your physical senses fuel lust and desire in men, not just how you look.

And it doesn't stop there. For desire to fully flower, it requires chemistry, trust, personality, compatibility, passion, mutual exploration, shared experiences, and a million other subtle factors.

So, yes, he digs that beautiful model with the teeny-weenie bikini on the cover of *Sports Illustrated*. And yes, he probably fantasizes about her. But in the end, she's an image firing on one of his senses. You fire on all five. That image has no emotional, psychological, or physical connection to him. You do. That image has not shared any meaningful experiences with him. You have.

And that's why he can look up from the magazine and say, "I think you're beautiful," and mean it. Do not confuse the height of the flame with the depth of the heat.

What Do Men Think About When They See You Naked?

It isn't unusual for women with low body esteem to think their man is fantasizing about a thinner woman, even as he's making mad passionate love to them.

You're giving men way too much credit and not enough cash. Here's what's really going on when your clothes come off:

What You're Thinking	What He's Thinking
"I better turn off the lights so he doesn't see my jiggly thighs."	"Where's that light switch? I want to see her beautiful legs."
"I feel fat. He probably thinks I'm a tub."	"There's a naked woman in my bed!"

What You're Thinking	What He's Thinking
"The only way this is going to happen is if I wear a camisole to hide my stomach."	"Wow, when's that coming off?"
"Oh my god! He's touching the pooch in my belly."	"I can't believe how hard I get when we get in this position."
"That's it! Tomorrow I start my diet."	"That's it! Just like that. Oooh, baby."
"I know he's fantasizing about a thinner woman."	"I don't want to come too soon. I better think about Mother Theresa."

Who Are You Going to Believe?

My point, and I do have one, is that you should approach the bedroom the way you approach a movie—with a willingness to suspend disbelief. You have to be willing to suspend your doubts about his attraction to your body. Don't be upset because the reflection in his eyes doesn't match the reflection you see in the mirror. Stop blaming him for the fact that you turn him on.

Preparing for the Sex Life You Deserve

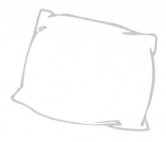

Let's look at how to prepare for that voodoo that you do…so much to avoid. First, we're going to talk about how you need to cultivate a consciousness of sensuality. I'm not talking about getting yourself in the mood for sex, but getting yourself in the mood for all kinds of pleasure, sexual or not.

Second, we'll take a look at what you can do about your low libido. Bedroom body anxiety tends to give libidos a flat tire. We need to get the blood flowing and the muscles toned so that you can regain the desire you used to have.

Third, you need to go on a geographic expedition of your own body. It's time for you to get acquainted or reacquainted with your likes, dislikes, and I-never-knew-I-likes. By understanding what turns you on and communicating it to your partner, you will put your inner critic on the horns of a dilemma: judgment or volcanic ecstasy?

Watch out for that lava.

5

CULTIVATING SENSUALITY IN AND OUT OF THE BEDROOM

"I've never spent a lot of money on fancy haircuts or mani-pedis. What's the point? It won't make any difference."
—Kara, 32, Cleveland, Ohio

The monkey chatter in your head prevents you from enjoying sex. It's a nonstop diatribe about your thighs being too big or your stomach not being as flat as an ironing board. It's punctuated by an obsession with your partner's opinion of your body and a compulsive search for the best way to hide perceived flaws. It takes over and prevents you from being in the moment and feeling pleasurable sensations. You may not be able to fully eliminate the monkey chatter, but you can give it a stutter, a lisp, and maybe even a gag order by cultivating sensuality outside the bedroom.

What I mean by cultivating sensuality is training your body to expect, appreciate, and flourish from sensory stimulation. Doing so trains you to pay more attention to what you're feeling than what you're thinking—something you might have problems doing in the bedroom.

My friend Shannon has a great outgoing voice mail message:

> Hi. I can't pick up the phone right now because I'm doing something I enjoy. I like doing it up and down, side to side, and all around. Sometimes I even like it a little rough. So I'll give you a call when I'm through... brushing my teeth.

Sensuality is a celebration of sensation. Any sensation, even the fresh feeling of brushing your teeth. If my girlfriend can express that much sensuality in something as mundane as dental hygiene, can you imagine how sensual she is in other areas of her life? It's no accident—sensuality warms the path to sexuality.

Cultivating sensuality is the enjoyment, expression, and—most importantly—pursuit of physically pleasing sensations. It's easy to dismiss it as simply pampering yourself or being mindful of your surroundings. That is definitely part of it, but we're aiming for something that directly addresses a major fault line in your sex life: your decreased ability to enjoy physical sensations because your mind is banging the gavel on your body. Sensuality in many ways is the practice of letting go of criticism and judgment and surrendering thought to feeling. You don't judge a bath towel when you feel its softness—you simply get lost in its softness.

When you began to live sensually, you cultivate gratitude for the pleasures your body can give you. But the most important thing about creating a space for pleasure is that it teaches you how to be in the moment. Pleasure—whether it's the smell of fresh coffee beans roasting or the breeze off the bay—directs your attention from your thoughts to your feelings.

The idea isn't to stop, smell the roses, and call it a day. It's to be conscious of pulling pleasure into your life on a daily basis. Mindfulness is certainly part of it. Yes, you should take the time to look up at the sky and notice the clouds. Yes, you should feel the thickness and texture of a fabric, a book, or a flower petal. Yes, you should take a languid bath. Yes, you should drink a cup of tea with your eyes closed. But what I'm talking about is far more than taking a minute out of your day to center yourself. It's about living a consciously sensual life. It's about looking at every aspect of your life and reordering it to throw out what doesn't give you pleasure and introduce things that do.

The connection between cultivating sensuality and improving sexuality is very real. The five senses create emotional states. The best way to improve your mood isn't to think pleasant thoughts; it's to rearrange your circumstances so that your body experiences something pleasurable. You can try to motivate yourself to go to the gym with positive thoughts all you want, but it'll be a lot more effective to play the kind of music that changes your mood. It's the same thing with sex. It's a lot easier to get and stay in the mood by firing up your senses than changing negative thoughts.

How to Increase Your Sensual Potential

Be brutal about your pleasure. If something is not making you happy, toss it out. If you open those drawers and those panties don't make you smile, get rid of them. Edit things out of your life that aren't sensually appealing. And make sure you never throw something out without replacing it.

Train yourself to stop whatever you're doing and ask, *How can I get more physical pleasure out of what I'm doing?* If you're reading a book, put it down for a second and add some ambiance by lighting a candle. If you're tired of walking into a room that depresses you, buy flowers. In fact, get a flower budget. The colors and fragrance will completely change your experience of the room. Don't wait for guys to buy you flowers. They only do it when they want something or have done something.

Insist on sensation. Demand on delight. Be merciless. Take your clothes as an example. Do they pull where they should lay? Sag where they should hold you up? Are they itchy? Do they make you feel good? No? Throw them out.

Don't worry about looking sexy

Cultivating sensuality isn't about making your body look the part; it's about making it feel the love, so don't worry about looking properly sexy. Instead, I want you to concentrate on picking out clothes that feel good against your skin. Want to look sexy? Fine, just don't wear clothes that pinch or itch. Want to look frumpy? Fine, as long as the baggy clothes make your skin dance in its softness. It's not a look we're going for; it's a feeling. Remember to always buy quality. Better to have one piece of clothing that feels luxurious against your skin than three that don't.

The nose knows

There's a reason why priests wave certain types of incense in a Catholic Mass. There's a reason why department store salespeople spritz perfume on you. Smells influence your emotions. Smells can attract or repel. It's important to have things that smell good on you and around you. Add fragrance to your environment—your car, bathrooms, office. Be surrounded by pleasant fragrances and your body will reward you with an uplifted mood.

Take inventory of what you like

You can probably recite which parts of your body you don't like in your sleep. But I bet you can't itemize the parts you like without scratching your head or rubbing your chin. If you're like a lot of women I know, you're probably thinking, "But I don't like any part of my body!" Trust me, you do. Studies show that even women with extreme body dissatisfaction can point to small things they like about themselves. Sometimes it's as simple as the shape of their fingers or the curls in their hair. If you honestly can't think of a single thing you like about yourself, you're still not off the hook. Pick things you feel neutral about.

Pamper what you like

Now that you've identified what you like (or feel neutral about), it's time to celebrate, nurture, and cultivate your best assets. For example, if you like the shape of your feet, you need to regularly treat yourself to a pedicure. If you like your hair, you need to buy the kind of products that make it shinier, fuller, curlier, or whatever it needs to enhance what it is you like about it. This isn't just about rewarding the body you've been punishing; it's about appreciating, cultivating, and experiencing sensuality. Remember, the goal isn't to make you feel better about your body; it's to make your body feel better things.

Two Simple Questions to Light Up Your Sex Life

Adding sensual pleasure to your everyday life requires an acute sense of awareness. No matter where you are or what you're doing, you should always pose this question: *How can I make my body feel better?* If you're in a cubicle at work, it could be as easy as putting soft music on. If you're tired, it could be a foot bath. It doesn't matter. Get yourself in the habit of asking, *How can I enhance the physical sensations I'm experiencing?* Because once you're in the habit of asking—and delivering—what feels good, you can transfer this skill to the bedroom. Of course, that won't do much good if your bedroom is so messy it looks like a crime scene.

Turning Your Bedroom into a Sensuous Lair

I am regularly shocked when I see how couples treat their bedrooms. They are often so filled with obstacles and diversions, it's a wonder that any sex could be had. Once, during *Sex Inspectors*, we talked to a couple in a bedroom that was so filled with clutter, I could hardly make out the bed. It reminded me of playing tennis with three chairs in the middle of the court. How are you supposed to hit the ball if there's always something in the way?

Too many people use their bedroom as if it were half storage unit, half entertainment center. The bedroom is for sleeping, relaxation, and sex. Anything that doesn't promote those three things needs to be moved out.

The energy in your bedroom can make the difference between putting you in the mood or locking you out of it. The point isn't to make it feel like sex is seeping out of the walls; it's to make your body feel relaxed, warm, and receptive to pleasure. We spend more time in our bedrooms than any other room in the house, yet it's often the most neglected.

From lighting to fragrances, you can have a bedroom that entices your body from the minute you walk in. Here are a few hints that can dramatically transform your experience of sex, love, and sleep. You know you've done a good job when you walk in and your body sighs with pleasure.

Lighting

The lighting in the perfect bedroom should generally be soft and low wattage. Consider installing a dimmer switch for your overhead light, so you can change the mood of the room easily. Colored or low-wattage bulbs will also help.

If you like lamps in your bedroom, use three-way light bulbs— that way you can read with the higher settings and set a mood with the lower ones. Experiment with lamps by putting them on the floor. The up-lighting gives off a nice glow. If you're feeling adventurous, mix things up with a strobe light—it can make your lovemaking look like a dream sequence.

Candles: the universal language of romance

Fire invokes romance, passion, and desire. It's primal. Nobody's mood stays the same when a candle gets lit. Earlier I said you need a flower budget. You need one for candles, too. Get out of the habit of thinking that lighting candles is for special occasions. Don't just light them as a precursor to making love or because you're enjoying a romantic dinner. Light them all the time for any sort of reason. Vary the sizes, colors, and placement. Train yourself to create different moods.

Use lots of reds (which stand for sexual attraction, passion, and love) and whites (which stand for personal power and romance). To symbolize a happy and close relationship, consider placing two candles close together. Mirrors can accentuate the lighting in your room. Enhance the glow of candles by placing them in front of or even on top of mirrors. On a side note, if you place a larger mirror on the wall opposite of a window, it will help reflect natural light and open the room up a bit.

Bedspread

The bedspread is probably the most important visual element in the bedroom because it takes up so much space. Don't go overboard with flashy designs or strong colors. Go with muted colors. Think romantic oasis, not flashy nightclub or botanical garden.

Floors

Wood floors are beautiful, but they're not soft. If wall-to-wall carpeting isn't feasible, then buy a wool-silk rug—with candlelight it creates a beautiful, shimmering effect. Stepping onto a shag or sheepskin rug by the foot of the bed feels great whether you're climbing into bed or getting out of it.

Windows and walls

Shut out the world with blackout curtains or a three-fold layered window treatment like wooden blinds and sheer curtains topped by floor-to-ceiling draperies. Generally speaking, the more fabric you put on walls and windows, the more soothing and sumptuous the room will be. Covering an entire wall with floor-to-ceiling drapes quiets the room in a provocative way.

Paint the walls a rich color and keep everything else in the room light and neutral. Choose body-flattering colors and avoid green or yellow. No one looks good in green reflection, and yellow makes you look jaundiced. Not a good look for sex!

Pillows

Women often make the mistake of over-pillowing the bed. While it may look good, it psychologically puts the bed off limits by taking up so much room. An over-pillowed bed sends a strong signal that the bed is a decorative prop rather than a place for communion. It is a subtle but unmistakable "do not lie here" sign. All you need are two sham-size pillows placed against the headboard and two to four sleeping pillows.

Bed linens

You want the sexiest tactile experience, which you can only get with thread counts starting at 450 to 1,000. Keep the sheets as plain as possible—no distracting designs or embroideries. Silk and satin feel awesome against your skin, but they do slide around and good luck getting the stains out. Try flannel sheets—they're cuddly and warm. Or try mixing bedding textures, like silk sheets with a satin pillow and a flannel blanket. Mix linens up so you're always experiencing something new and exciting.

Scenting your bed sheets is a great way to enhance a sexual ambiance. Try the following:

- Add several drops of your favorite aromatherapy oil to the softener section of your washing machine. Or put the drops in a small cotton handkerchief or washcloth and throw it in the dryer with your bed linens.

- Spray your sheets with a sheet scent spray, such as "Smooth as Velvet."
- Pour a quarter-cup of scented bath salts in the final rinse cycle. Or throw a tied-up washcloth filled with salts in the dryer to tumble along with the bed sheets.
- Scent a washcloth or small piece of fabric with your favorite perfume or essential oil and throw it in the dryer with the bedding.
- Dust some Kama Sutra Honey Dust between your sheets. Honey dust absorbs perspiration and won't get sticky like a lot of powders.
- Fill a spray bottle with water and add a few drops of your favorite essential oil and then spray it on your sheets.

The bed itself

Add a romantic canopy or tent, even if you're not sleeping in a four-poster bed. You can simply hang it from the ceiling with eye hooks.

If you have plain-looking curtains, try spicing things up a bit by replacing them with billowy, lacy curtains. These look terrific, and if you have a quiet, low-speed fan in the room, the curtains will sway back and forth, creating a billowy motion.

Soundtrack your love life

Besides lighting, nothing creates an atmosphere and maintains the mood more than music. Make sure the entire stereo, not just the speakers, is in the bedroom. There's nothing worse than leaving the room to change the CD.

Kick your romance quotient up a notch or two by burning your own playlist. If you want to go classical, you can't go wrong with

Making Out to Mozart, *Shacking Up to Chopin*, or *Bedroom Bliss With Beethoven*. If you want something more contemporary, try some of the seductive vibes in *Ultra Chilled* CDs.

Fragrances

Typically, a couple's bedroom is fragrant with female scents—perfumes, sprays, and colognes. But in your case you should consider scenting the room with a more masculine scent. Specifically, lavender. French studies reveal that women respond more favorably to men in rooms scented with lavender.

Bedroom Don'ts

If you want your bedroom to be sexy, clean it. Laundry piled on the dresser, mountains of loose change, and dirty clothes on the floor are enough to make a Viagra pill go soft. Anything that doesn't promote a romantic or relaxing atmosphere has to go, including...

Pictures

No photos of the family. When your partner yells "WHO'S YOUR DADDY!" he doesn't want to be looking at a picture of your father. It'll just confuse him.

And please, no pictures of ex-boyfriends. They're okay for one-night stands, but if you actually know the name of the guy you brought home (a good sign you want to date him), then ditch the ex pics.

Pets

It's okay to have an animal in the bedroom if it's you on all fours. Otherwise, keep them out. Do you really want your cat coughing up a hairball when you reach the moment of truth? Or a dog that pokes you with a cold wet nose in an inappropriate spot? Close the door on Fido and Frida.

Clutter

Papers, clips, staplers, pens, dirty laundry, clean laundry, keys, spare change, *please*. Nothing kills a romantic mood faster than clutter. If you have a small bedroom, just eliminating clutter can make it look a lot bigger. Have a designated storage space (a decorative box for instance) for spare change, papers, and anything else that's cluttering the room.

Miscellaneous items

Laundry: If it absolutely can't go anywhere but the bedroom, at least keep it in a shut hamper without stray socks or sweaters hanging out of it.

Exercise equipment: Another bad idea in the bedroom. There is nothing romantic, relaxing, or soothing about something that looks like a medieval torture device NASA threw out of the shuttle.

Television: It's a WMD—a weapon of mass distraction. Take it out of the room, unless you're going to watch an erotic video together. If you can't bring yourself to do it, how about a compromise? Hide your television (and other electronic equipment) inside a large armoire, so it doesn't take away from the romantic look of your room.

Bedroom Do's

There are three items you might consider putting in your bedroom:

An aquarium: It's relaxing and adds a touch of nature.

A tabletop fountain or waterfall: Water is symbolic for renewal.

An upholstered bench: It tends to make the bed bigger and more inviting.

From Sensuality to Sexuality

Remember, there is a point to all this emphasis on sensuality. We are addressing the fact that your appearance anxiety interferes with your ability to feel pleasure in bed. Cultivating sensuality is a gag order on the monkey chatter. It trains your mind to take a backseat to your body. It keeps you in the moment and out of your thoughts.

Cultivating sensuality means training yourself to be aware of what your body likes. By giving yourself fully to the sensation of pleasure, you bypass your inner critic. By emphasizing the primacy of your senses, your body can reset the wiring in your mind. Remember, our first-order goal is to enhance your sense of well-being, which promotes sex, which reinforces well-being, which increases sexual desire. Cultivating sensuality on a daily basis will pull you into this reinforcement cycle, which ultimately takes the chatter out of the monkey.

When you allow your body to experience joy, you gain a better appreciation of it. You will do things for it the way it does things for you. The mind-body connection is a dance. You've been letting your mind take the lead, and all it's done is step on toes, wrench backs, and move the wrong ways. It's time to let your body take over for a little while. It's a wonderful partner when you learn to follow its lead.

TUNE IN SO YOU CAN TURN ON

"After a while you just get exhausted from the constant self-criticism about your body and give up. I've cut myself off from my emotions to the point that sometimes I don't even know what I'm feeling."

—Laura, 40, Bellevue, Illinois

Have you ever seen a speaker tap a microphone that's obviously working and ask, "Is this thing on?" That's actually what happens with body-conscious women. All the physiological signs of arousal are at work, but they still ask themselves, "Am I turned on?"

Women who are dissatisfied with their bodies are less able to accurately estimate heartbeat, blood glucose levels, and muscle contractions. This tends to create a greater disconnect between the physical signs of arousal (rapid heartbeat, muscle tension, etc.) and your subjective experience of it ("Am I turned on?"). In other words, your fires may be stoking, but you can't sense the heat.

In this chapter we are going to close the gap between your physiologic response and your subjective awareness, and we're going to do it with a mirror, a hand, and a vibrator. Yes, we're going to chart your erotic terrain. It's only by understanding what your body responds to and how it responds that you'll be able to pick up on its subtleties, interpret them correctly, and act on them appropriately.

In chapter five, we saw how awareness of, respect toward, and attention to your body's desires improves your sense of well-being. It's no different in bed. Let's apply the skills we learned in cultivating sensuality and make it work in the bedroom. It all starts by asking yourself the mother of all sex questions: *Do I like it like this or like that?*

All Hands on Deck

Women with bedroom body shame tend to have a one-way relationship with their bodies. They speak and their bodies listen. It's time to switch roles. Listen and let your body speak. It has a lot to say, and believe me, you're going to love what you hear.

Your body has lots of pleasure zones. Some are obvious, some aren't. Your job is to find out what's hot and what's not. There's no better way to do that than to be, as Jerry Seinfeld once bragged, "the master of your own domain."

Let's say you discover your orgasms are much more powerful if you avoid directly stimulating your clitoris and focus on the area slightly below it. You not only discovered something pleasurable, but you also gained a profound understanding of how your body works and, in turn, gained mastery over it. You'll gain new respect (and wonder) at your body and be more willing to share it with the person you love.

Filling Yourself Out Like an Application

The best way of "listening" to your body is to "map out" your hot spots. You'll see lots of techniques in the following pages, but they're essentially variations of a three-step process—hauling out a hand, a vibrator, and asking the same question you learned in cultivating sensuality: *How can I make this more physically pleasurable?*

By understanding how your body responds to touch, pressure, temperature, moisture, positions, fantasies, and environment, you will become more confident in bed. It will be easier to sense the signs of physiological arousal, act on it, and, just as importantly, communicate it to your partner. Believe me, he wants to know. Knowing how to turn on a woman is a man's biggest turn-on.

Unless it's mind-blowing oral. But we'll get to that in the next chapter.

Mapping the Goods

The problem with most body-conscious women is that they've spent so much time covering or avoiding their body they've never actually taken a good look at their pleasure center. It's hard to conduct erotic cartography when you're too embarrassed to look at the map.

Some studies suggest that nearly 30 percent of women have never examined their own vulvas in the mirror. It's a good bet that a majority of women with appearance anxiety have never done it. So haul out a hand mirror, ladies; we're going to do a little aerial reconnaissance.

I will leave you to decide how to conduct the guided tour of your personal landscape. The goal isn't to become an anatomical expert as much as to familiarize yourself with the location, look, and power of different joy-joy zones, from the outer third of the vagina (where most of the sensitive nerve endings reside) to the clitoral glans to the G-spot.

Look at your genitals by spreading your legs and using a mirror. Lie down on your back or sit up. Put your feet up against the wall or squat. There is no "correct" position. Explore yourself. You're not there to see if you like the look of your vulva (if you're a lifelong practitioner of body shame, it's a safe bet you won't) but to understand what it looks like, to make it more real for you. Just like looking at yourself in the makeup mirror gives you a sense of your personhood, looking at your vulva gives you a sense of your sexual self. Don't judge; *notice.*

Explore with the mirror several times over the next couple of weeks. Shock and shame may dominate the first session as you're not accustomed to seeing body parts that are almost always covered up. It's only in subsequent sessions that those feelings attenuate, affording you a better sense of how you're put together. If you're like most women, you're going to be initially surprised by the size, shape, color, and texture of different areas of the vulva. Some of your discoveries will be pleasing, some won't. Try not to judge. Notice.

What's Your Pleasure?

Now that you have a better understanding of your landscape, let's see what rich ores lie beneath. It's time to test-drive your vulva. Set some time when you can be alone, away from any distractions, including your partner. This is about you and you, not you and him. Prepare your self-pleasuring sessions with a little shopping expedition. Buy lubricants with different textures and smells. Consider using videos or reading sexually arousing stories to eroticize the context.

It bears repeating that if you can't sense the physiological signs of your arousal, if you don't figure out what you like and don't like (and communicate it to your partner), sex will remain a chore instead of a choice. But the more important reason to follow the recommendations you're about to read is that masturbation primes the body's sexual plumbing. Pleasuring yourself regularly creates a cycle of craving that amps up your libido and warms the path to partner sex.

Ready, set, explore. Stroke the clitoris, touch the labia majora, caress the perineum. Get a sense of ownership and agency of your body. Experiment with different kinds of touch. Harder, softer, quicker, slower. Every woman is different—there is no right way to do this, only your way. A lot of women are partial to gently and rhythmically rubbing the clitoris with a finger or two, slowly increasing the intensity. Others like to stroke the area around the clitoris, and still others like to put pressure on the areas above and below it—the pubic bone and urethra.

Try combining this with manual stimulation in and around the vagina. Rub up and down, back and forth, around and round in different directions. Experiment with different speeds and pressure. Don't forget to stimulate the area in and around your anus. Tighten and loosen your pelvic floor muscles while you're doing all this. Try crossing your legs and exerting rhythmic pressure on your genital area. Rock your pelvis. Breathe deeply. Relax. You're not a lab rat, and this is not a science experiment. Listen to your body. What does it want? What does it respond to? How is it reacting?

Women may have the same parts, but they don't have the same number of nerve endings in those parts. That's why what turns your friends on may turn you off. Breast play, for example, can bring you to orgasm or bore you to tears. It all depends on the concentration of nerve endings in your breasts.

Don't use a vibrator until you've done this exercise a few times. Vibrators are healthy ways to get stronger stimulation, but skin-to-skin contact is the best way of gaining mastery, competence, confidence, and comfort in what your body responds to. Once you feel at ease with your fingers doing the walking, you can graduate to motorized stimulation.

Put Your Phone On Vibrate

If Cleopatra could find something to pleasure herself, so can you. A curator of New York's Museum of Sex says there's evidence the Egyptian queen kept a hard-shelled gourd filled with bees for use as a primitive vibrator. She literally took the sting out of masturbation.

Now, you don't have to go to those lengths, but it wouldn't hurt to become a busy little bee and do some field research. So go to an adult toy store or shop online and buy a range of products made with different materials, speeds, and power. Plastic vibrators are popular because they're terrific at transferring vibrations, but some women prefer vibrators made from jelly because they're softer and more flexible. Others like silicone because of the higher quality material and varied textures.

You may have given up on some good vibrators because you didn't try them with the speed and pressure that turns you on. Consider electric vibrators. They're far more powerful than battery-operated toys. True, you have to plug them in, but maybe it's time to put a little *vrrrooom* in your room.

How to Shop for a Sex Toy

Buying sex toys is a little like opening a Christmas present—you never know whether you're going to like it until you open the package, and then it's too late. Only a few companies give you a satisfaction guarantee, and I'm not aware of any "try-out" rooms before you buy. And you can't exactly borrow your friend's vibrator (and if you can, you may have to rethink your friendships).

This doesn't mean you can't improve the chances of getting what you like the first time. After your hand-driven self-pleasuring sessions, you should know the kind of stimulation that turns you on. This will narrow down your options. For example, if inserting your fingers into your vagina doesn't do much for you, then you can eliminate penis-size dildos made for vaginal insertion.

Sex toys aren't made for different types of people; they're made for different types of stimulation. There are basically three things a sex toy can help you with: external stimulation, penetration, or both.

How Much Do You Want to Spend?

There isn't always a correlation between quality and pleasure. An inexpensive sex toy can be just as much fun as a luxury toy, but it probably won't last as long. Once you know what you like, I do recommend investing in high-end sex toys as they are less wasteful and often have better designs. But to start off with, unless you've got a lot of money to spend, I recommend sticking with budget toys until you know what you want. There's nothing worse than spending $130 on a sex toy that ends up as a jewelry tree.

Getting the Most Out of Your Toys

Whatever you pick, try the toys in different positions. What makes you yawn on your back may make you howl on your stomach. Try some lubrication, too.

Do you have areas that are too sensitive to touch with a vibrator? Some women find their nipples and clitoris too sensitive for direct stimulation. Try a "brush-by," a light glide that barely touches them. Try stimulating yourself on one side of the clitoris as opposed to the other. If you're particularly sensitive, do it through your panties and gradually your body will be able to tolerate more and more direct stimulation.

You can also drape a hand towel over your genitals to diffuse the intensity. Just make sure you don't wipe off your natural vaginal lubrication. It'll cause redness, irritation, and sometimes burning.

Use your other hand to stimulate at the same time. You might find, for example, that stimulating your nipples while the vibrator stimulates your clitoris sends you reeling into deep space. And move your hips and body rhythmically as you do all of this. One last thing: don't hold your breath. You'll experience more by breathing fully.

Multifactor your self-pleasuring. Use fantasy, erotic books, videos, even memories of mind-blowing sex, as you tour your personal landscape. Don't separate the physical from the emotional or psychological. Your body responds to all stimulants in a way that's greater than the sum of its parts.

Tongue-Tied in Bed?

It's time to communicate what kind of stimulation makes you hear colors. Tell your partner what kind of touch, kiss, or stroke makes the difference between hearing pastels and primary colors. What kind of speed, pressure, and friction do you need? He needs to know if playing with your nipples does anything for you, and, if so, what exactly he needs to pay attention to. He needs to know when, how far, what angle, and how fast you want him inside you. He needs you to guide the pacing and the depth of his thrusts. He needs to know all of this and more because, well, and I say this with love, what men don't know about women is a lot.

Men learn how to pleasure women by watching porn and listening to each other in the locker room. I don't know which source should scare you more. Almost all porn ignores or deliberately misrepresents female sexuality to center around male needs. Add the ill-informed, locker-room mentality ("Chicks love it when you pull their braids thug-style") and you've got, well, a lot of work cut out for you. Even guys who've been with lots of women aren't necessarily good in bed. Not if the women were too shy, fearful, or intimidated to let them know what they needed.

The good news is that most guys *want* to know how to pleasure women. As long as you don't frame your request as an insult or a demand, or lace it with sarcasm, as if he should know better, you have a great shot at shaping him into being the lover you always dreamed of.

There are few things that exemplify male ignorance or confusion about sex more than intercourse. Typically, men get more enjoyment from it than women because the penis gets direct stimulation, while the clitoris doesn't. Men (and a lot of women) are taught that the vagina is the primary sexual organ and greatest source of sexual pleasure for women. This adds up to a steaming hot plate of cluelessness: confusion on a bed of unfamiliarity with a side of uncertainty. *There's* a meal where everybody goes home hungry. He may not know that he (or you) should manually stimulate the clitoris during intercourse, and you may be too shy, reserved, or intimidated to tell him.

Communication leads you to the all-you-can-eat buffet. Once everybody's clear on what everybody likes and how to deliver it, everybody goes home full. The question is, how do you communicate a delicate matter without it being taken the wrong way?

Good lovers are born, not made.
If your partner really loved you, he'd know what you like.
You shouldn't have to tell him things that are so obvious.

These three sentences are the kinds of misinformed beliefs that can stop sex in its tracks. Guys aren't born with a vagina and a clitoris— they know about as much about the vulva as you do about the penis. Less, actually, because male sexuality is a lot less complicated.

And it's not like they can ask. The male ego is like a giant skyscraper built on a landfill. Nothing will open up the ground faster than admitting ignorance about something "real men" are supposed to know. Men think it's better to pretend you know what you're doing than to admit you don't. That's why waiting for a guy to ask what you like is like waiting for him to ask a stranger for directions. It's possible, but by the time it happens you'll be making a left in Middle Earth.

So, unless you have an enlightened male, it's pretty much up to you to initiate sexual communication. Fortunately, it's not very hard or even awkward to do if you follow a few rules:

Show, don't tell

Hands communicate better than words. If you want him to touch you a certain way, gently guide his hand and say, "I really like it like this."

Reward his behavior

When he's doing it the way you like, exaggerate your pleasure by moaning or groaning a little louder, kissing him a bit harder, and drawing him in closer.

Don't reject, redirect

If he's touching an area that isn't doing it for you, don't push his hand away; redirect it to its rightful spot. It's okay to pull back slightly, wiggle away, or even say "ouch" if it hurts, as long as you guide him.

Tell him what you want more of, not less of

Don't tell him he kisses you like he's committing a felony, tell him you love it when his tongue presses gently but firmly against yours (if that's what you like). And always end a request with these two words: "*Like this.*" And show him how.

You Want WHAT?

Speaking of communication, you'll need lots of it if you have a partner who might be insulted at the thought of bringing vibrators into your playpen when that's something you want to do.

Men don't understand why women like to use inanimate objects to deepen sexual pleasure. We don't need them so we sometimes we have a hard time accepting why you do. We don't have mysterious pleasure zones whose very existence is up for debate (like the G-spot). And we don't know what to do with a vibrating device, except to stuff it in the DVD player to cool it after playing nonstop porn.

The truth is, sex toys are nothing but motorized masturbation. If he doesn't mind you masturbating, he shouldn't mind you motorizing it. Typically, the best way to a man's heart is through his eyes—by allowing him to watch you masturbate with the toy. You can't go wrong by giving men a chance to *Wow, you mean I get to watch?!!!!* Or by appealing to their discriminating sense of *Can you do that thing again?* Or his selfless desire to *Don't move, I need more lube!*

Typically, that takes care of the problem, but if you're too self-conscious to let him watch, you need to take a different approach. A lot of men think sex toys are an indictment on their ability to satisfy women, and they can become quite paranoid about it. They'll misinterpret everything you say. "I want to spice things up" means you think his penis is too small. "We'll discover new horizons in pleasure" means you're squinting, then rolling your eyes at it. And "I want to have deeper orgasms" means you're thinking you would've been better off dating his brother.

Fortunately, it's the rare man who can't be turned around with a little reassurance. Just poke a hole in the myths. No, sex toys aren't part of your nefarious Penis Replacement Plan. No, you're not going to get addicted and join a twelve-step program because the G-spot finder made your life unmanageable. Yes, you'll leave him for a pair of AA batteries—as soon as they plug into something that kisses and holds you like he does.

And yes, even the best carpenters use power tools.

The Power of Knowing What You Like

Studies confirm that body-conscious women have a harder time recognizing physiologic arousal. They're less likely to notice or process it as the initial stages of sexual desire. By surveying your landscape and testing its boundaries, you'll get definitive answers to what you like and what turns you on. You'll not only be better able to recognize the physical signs of arousal, but also create and heighten them. You'll also set the stage for better sex by communicating your needs to your partner, who can then take over and take you places you can't get by yourself.

Of course, recognizing early-stage arousal is important. But what if your newly tuned radar doesn't pick up on anything because there's nothing there? What if you can't sense the heat because the fire never got lit? As you're about to read, libido is sometimes a do-it-yourself job.

7

NOVEL WAYS OF RAISING YOUR LIBIDO

"I'm in a sexless marriage. After years of hiding my body and coming up with excuses to avoid sex, I think my husband just gave up. I feel like I have no connection to my body or to him. I want to want it, but I don't know how to make it happen."

—Sandi, 45, Dallas, Texas

If you've been struggling with body consciousness in the bedroom, your libido probably went south and opened up a darling boutique hotel somewhere near the equator. Low libido is common among the body conscious. If you see sex as an opportunity to be shamed, your body probably responds in three ways: It lowers your desire for sex, it decreases your ability to pick up and act on "erotic cues" (like that flutter in your stomach when you smell your partner's cologne), and reduces pleasurable sensations when you actually do make love.

And so the avoidance game that we've talked about so much begins. You find yourself going to bed earlier or later than your partner so you don't have to face the possibility of his advances. Or you lie still in bed, pretending you're asleep, so he won't touch you.

You start making excuses that sound reasonable: You're too tired for sex, the kids will walk in on you, you have a lot on your mind. You become defensive. You tell him if he worked as hard as you did he wouldn't want sex either. Besides, didn't you just have sex a couple of nights ago? Whatever. He's a sex maniac. He doesn't want you, he just wants sex and you're the closest person around. If he just appreciated you more for all the housework you do. Besides, he's not even that good of a lover.

These are the kind of thoughts that low-libido women use to form a man moat, foiling the most adept swimmers from reaching the castle. Some of your observations may be true (you probably are fatigued), but they still keep you stuck in a place you'd rather not be. But let's put you on pause for a moment while we talk about…

What the Lack of Sex Is Doing to Him

For men, intimacy is oxygen. Cut it off and you turn your partner into a sexual asthmatic—chronically coughing and wheezing in his attempt to breathe you in. He'll experience a tightening of the chest and eventually his lips turn blue (among other organs).

Make no mistake, when you constantly reject your partner's advances with some version of "I have clothes to fold," he hears it as "I don't love you." Or want you. So go away.

For men, sex equals love. A lack of touch leads to emotional scurvy. When love, which used to flow freely, gets harder to come by, it's hard not to turn the rejection against yourself. They believe they're to blame, that they're no longer attractive, that their manhood is useless, their desire is pointless, and that their needs are unworthy.

If your unwillingness to have sex continues long enough, he'll grow distant and angry, which then *really* puts you off sex. But his negativity is an understandable reaction to having love withdrawn. His anger is a manifestation of the hurt that lies underneath. He feels punished for something he didn't do. The effect of the punishment causes pain; the unjustness causes anger. It's hard for you to see this, of course, because now you're reacting to his self-defensive distance and anger, rather than his understandable hurt. Rejecting his sexual advances makes him suspicious, insecure, inadequate, vulnerable, hurt, resentful, and unloved. And it's especially easy for him to think you're cheating on him. The rationale goes something like this: "She has a great body and it turns me on. Yet she claims that she's too embarrassed about her body to have sex. The same body that gives me raging hard-ons! I think she's lying and that she's using it as an excuse because she's seeing somebody else."

It isn't just that the most powerful expression of love got taken away from him. Sex is a proxy for a man's self-esteem and masculinity. It's a platform for confidence and virility. There's not much room for masculinity and virility when you're reduced to nagging and negotiating for sex, or being the only one initiating it or knowing your partner is merely tolerating it.

Once during the filming of *The Sex Inspectors*, I sat on a bed with a woman I was advising (don't worry, we were fully clothed—it wasn't that kind of show!). The video cameras that we put throughout her house showed how cruelly she rejected her husband's affections. I said, "Put your arm around me; I want to show you how you reject your husband." I whacked it away like a horsefly just landed on me and looked away from her. Indignantly, she said, "I do *not* do that!" I said, "Yes, you do." She knew I was right. I could see her face softening. I leaned in. "Can I tell you a secret?" She nodded. I cupped my hand around her ear and whispered something. She started bawling. The producer, director, and audio people went nuts because the microphone didn't pick up what I said. The director stopped the filming to give the woman time to compose herself, took me aside, and asked, "What the hell did you say to make her cry like that?"

I said, "*Men have feelings, too.*"

My point in bringing all this up isn't to make you feel guilty; it's to make you understand the consequences of your withdrawal. Reversing the damage will take some work, and you need to be highly motivated, not by guilt but by love—for the man in your life and your own sense of who you are and what you're capable of growing into. Nobody should take a vow of sexual poverty when they date or get into a relationship. Especially you.

How You Lost Your Will to Have Sex

When shame walks in the door, lust flies out the window. Women with healthy body consciousness treat their natural desires as welcome guests. They open the door, take their coat, hand them a drink, and welcome them into the living room where the fragrance of a gourmet meal wafts in from the kitchen. The message is clear: You are welcome. *Mi casa es su casa.*

Women with noticeably bad body esteem treat their natural desires as unwelcome guests who muddy the carpets and eat all the pretzels. They stand by the door and say, "Here's your hat, what's your hurry?"

What's causing this low libido? I want you to consider something that may never have occurred to you: Your loss of libido is a coping strategy that your mind uses to protect itself from experiencing shame. What appears to you as a baffling lack of desire is actually a subconscious decision on your part to get rid of it so you don't experience more hurt.

Basically, you have an internal conflict between your conscious desire ("I want to *want* to have sex") and your subconscious unwillingness ("If I have sex, he will see how fat I am, lose his erection, and stop loving me. He'll make fun of me or fantasize about skinnier women. I don't want to see the disappointment in his face when he sees my thighs jiggle or my stomach pooch out. *I will die of embarrassment.*").

Really, it's lousy self-talk when you're making love.

Somewhere along the line, your subconscious decided the best way to protect you from more pain was to reduce or eliminate your desires. Or rather, push them so far down that they seem undetectable. Remember, "subconscious" means below the level of conscious awareness. You're not aware that you made the decision, but you can certainly see the effects of it.

The solution? Bring your subconscious thoughts to awareness. Understand the decision your subconscious made in order to protect you. Start by reframing your thinking from *I want but I can't* to *I want but I won't*.

This isn't some pop psychology/build-it-and-they-will-come nonsense. There's a big difference between *can't* (an inability) and *won't* (an unwillingness). I know it doesn't make sense that you'd be unwilling to do what you desperately want, but you only have to look at the millions of men who struggle with an inability to ejaculate during intercourse to see a parallel. They want to ejaculate. Their penis is rock hard. They're able to do it when they're alone, but they just can't do it when they're having intercourse. They're fighting your fight: a conscious desire subverted by a subconscious fear.

If you want your libido to "come back," you have to consciously "undecide" a subconsciously made decision. You have to stop believing the demonstrably false assumption that your partner is going to be repulsed by what he sees and stop loving you or mortify you with disappointment and ridicule. You have to stop believing that sex is an opportunity to be shamed and start believing it's a springboard to a stronger emotional connection with the man you love. You have to believe that sex doesn't cut you up into a million pieces, that, in fact, it makes you whole.

Consciously undoing a subconscious decision is hard work. Luckily, you're going to be ably assisted with some special tactics proven to lift your libido. To start, it's important that you stop ignoring a certain sound at your door.

Knock, Knock. Who's There?

Not only does pronounced body consciousness seem to make your libido disappear, but it also makes you less able to detect it during the rare times it does make an appearance. Women with low body esteem are less likely to pay attention to, accurately identify, and therefore act on the physical sensations of arousal like a quickening pulse, muscle tension, and blood flow. Again, this is because your subconscious is trying to protect you from the anxiety and shame of disrobing.

Sex is the physical expression of your need for emotional intimacy, love, union, and partnership, a tangible way for you to give something of yourself. Typically, the desire for it appears at your door as a loud, insistent knock. Over time, your mind has learned to block its sounds. Occasionally, it opens the door, treats this longing as an unwanted vacuum cleaner salesman, and tells it to go away.

But your body insists so the knocking continues. The mind goes into pretend mode. It thinks, "Knocking, what knocking? It's the tree branches bumping together." It's not long before the body, weakened by a lack of nurturing, knocks softer and softer, to the point that it becomes so faint your mind doesn't have to ignore it or pretend it isn't there—it truly doesn't hear it.

For the most part, the knocking never really goes away. Just because you can't hear it clearly doesn't mean it's not there. Your job is twofold: to be on the lookout for the knocking when it comes and create the environment so that it will.

I Don't Feel a Thing

Body consciousness creates two types of libidinal depressions: low libido or low sensation. With low libido, you don't want it, you don't think about it, you don't fantasize about it, you're not even receptive to it.

With low sensation, you may think about it, you may want it, you may be receptive to it, but your body doesn't react the way it used to. It's a classic case of "the spirit is willing but the flesh is weak." There's a measurable lack of lubrication, decreased nipple sensitivity, and reduced clitoral and labial sensation or engorgement. There is also a lack of vaginal lengthening, dilation, and arousal.

While low libido/low sensation are clearly linked to emotional causes (stress, depression, watching the city fix potholes), there are physiological culprits, too: surgery, hormonal changes, underactive thyroid, alcohol, pregnancy, medications, and trauma.

None of my recommendations for jump-starting your libido will work if you have such an underlying physical condition. Start eliminating the possibilities by looking in your medicine cabinet. Any drug that affects your hormones, nerves, or blood circulation has the potential to make you able to say "no" to sex in eight different languages. Everyone knows antidepressants can let the air out of the libidinal balloon, but did you know that popular over-the-counter drugs like Tagamet, Zantac, Benadryl, and Aleve have the potential to do it, too? If you suspect there might be a physiological component to your low libido/low sensation, wiggle your index finger and dial your doctor. Otherwise, let's assume that you're low libido/low sensation is caused by stress—that you're so anxious about making love, you're making your coffee nervous.

A Word about Alcohol

Alcohol mugs libidos. It sneaks up behind you, knocks you to the ground, and steals your valuables. It relieves you of your libido and absconds with your performance. Alcohol metabolizes in the liver, which is also responsible for metabolizing testosterone, a crucial sex hormone. Too much liquor and your liver may start converting your testosterone to estrogen, contributing to a loss of sex drive. Alcohol also dulls the nerves that transmit sensations and decreases the body's ability to pump blood around the genitals, which is critical to sexual functioning.

Still, I feel your pain. Sex kittens don't drink milk. It's hard to imagine a romantic dinner without at least a glass of wine. Advising moderation is fine, but how much is too much? A study at Southern Illinois University showed three and a half drinks for a 150-pound person starts getting in the way. Every measure of arousal the researchers looked at went south after three and a half drinks.

The good news about alcohol is that it tends to relax you and melt away reservation, inhibition, and worry, the absence of which makes for great sex. So yes, alcohol is great for sex, until it isn't. Stay away from alcohol as much as you can for the next few months. Nobody likes to be "chemically inconvenienced," but drinking moderately or not at all will be a big help.

A Word about Smoking

If you smoke like the catalytic converter just went out on your muffler, you're going to reduce your sex life to ashes. Nicotine constricts blood vessels, which leads to hardening of the arteries. As your arteries become harder and narrower, they let less blood into your genitals, making it harder to get in the mood, enjoy sex, or achieve orgasm.

Quitting reverses the process, but not without some side effects along the way. It's not unusual for people who quit to temporarily feel mentally unfocused, sexually unsettled, or suffer a temporary loss of libido. If the problems persist, talk to your doctor about nicotine-replacement therapy to help ease the transition.

How to Raise Your Libido

Desire tends to express itself naturally. You normally don't have to think about it because it thinks for you. But for low-libido women, desire is a decision. It's a conscious intention to discover and learn new ways of keeping sexual energy alive. Obviously, you can't *decide* to be aroused, but you can *decide* to do things that lead to arousal. For example, if you're tense, you can't "decide" to relax, but you can "decide" to take deep breaths and consciously relax your muscles, which results in relaxation. Similarly, you can't "decide" to be sexually aroused, but you can decide to exercise, create an environment conducive to sex, follow the recommendations in this chapter, and set the stage for arousal to appear. Desire is like a flower: sometimes it blooms without effort, and sometimes you have to tend the earth to create the opportunity for the petals to spread.

Don't Wait for the Mood to Strike: Strike the Mood

Imagine going to the gym only when you felt like it. You'd get so out of shape you'd break your nose doing a push-up. To prevent that from happening, most people have a routine—they knock back an energy drink, crank up the music, and do a few warm-ups. Just like women figure out how to get themselves to the gym when they don't feel like exercising, you've got to figure out how to get yourself to bed when you don't feel like making love. You can't wait for the feeling to come up. You have to come up with the feeling.

But wait. Why should you come up with the feeling if it doesn't come up on its own? Isn't there something wrong with a relationship that requires you to conjure up desire as if you were a medium conjuring spirits in a séance? No, there isn't. There's something wrong with your understanding of sexual response. Let me explain.

Sexual response works in different ways for different people. High-libido people don't have to wait for a thought, a feeling, or a situation to get turned on. They're basically hormones with feet. They're so highly attuned to their bodies' responses that they act on the slightest hint of arousal. They don't have to bring forth sexual thoughts or fantasies because they come without effort. Low-libido people are the opposite. They tend to wait until they're flooded with feelings before they act. They interpret the absence of dramatic stirrings as proof they have little or no sexual desire.

But that is a falsehood, a grave misreading of how sexual response works. It's true that sexual desire is often unbidden. It just appears. But it's also true that it is bidden. It appears because *you called it forth*. In other words, you can wait for the feeling or you can come up with the feeling.

How "Cuing" Revs Up Low Libidos

Sometimes even basic biological drives need what psychologists call "cuing" to get them to surface to awareness. Take hunger, for example. Sometimes you're so busy and distracted that you forget to eat. But a cue will remind you. It can come in the form of looking at your watch and realizing you should have eaten hours ago or smelling freshly baked bread. Cues don't create desire, they remind you of them.

Situational cues act as triggers for an appropriate response. A change in lighting signals the start of a show. A sound effect is the cue for an actor to say his line. A gesture by a conductor signals a new direction in the music. Your partner's smell may be the cue for sexual stirring.

A cue is a prompt. A stimulus, either consciously or unconsciously perceived, that elicits or signals a type of behavior. It can be artificially set or organically grown. A cue can work accidentally (somebody walking by with a fresh batch of cookies) or on purpose (setting an alarm to remind you to eat). Sex drives can be "cued" in much the same way.

First, you have to understand what prompts a sexual response from you. Is it seeing romantic films? Watching erotic movies? Hearing a deep, resonant, sexually confident male voice? Sniffing an especially appealing aftershave? Picking up on a man's natural scent? Is it a long-lasting look into a man's eyes? (If you're wondering why that can be so powerful, it's because a look-lock releases phenylethylamine, a chemical that accelerates attraction. Some call this the copulatory gaze.)

Cues trigger a response that brings your desires to conscious awareness. And from there, your self-imposed chastity belt tends to unbuckle naturally. The challenge is to understand what your sexual cues are so they can trigger a response.

Below is a list of common sex cues. This is not a comprehensive list, as every woman is different, but it's a starting point. If you don't know whether something is a sexual cue for you, find out. For example, if you've never read erotic stories, buy them and see if your panties don't float to the floor.

Sex Cues

- Watching romantic movies
- Viewing soft or hard porn (especially made-for-women films)
- Reading erotic books or stories
- Hearing a resonant male voice
- Smelling a favorite aftershave
- Smelling a man's natural scent
- Seeing a man dominate (in sports, business, or sex)
- Consciously fantasizing about sex
- Talking dirty
- Doing something physical that gets you in touch with your body: sun bathing, dancing, exercising, playing a sport
- Affection (hugs, kisses, holding hands)
- Showering together
- A heart-to-heart talk with your date or partner

Context Makes Cues More Powerful

You can give your sexual cues more horsepower by providing them with a cue-friendly context. If a cue like reading erotic stories makes you hot, reading it in a crowded subway probably won't. But reading it alone under a soft light while listening to chill-out music is a horse of a different color. Or a man on a horse of a different color, depending on your erotic preferences.

Identify, Cultivate, and Engage Your Turn-Ons

Don't make the mistake of thinking that a cue is not a cue unless it drenches you with desire. You don't need a downpour; a sprinkle will do. Low-libido women tend to wait until they're overwhelmed with desire to act on it. This is a mistake, first because you'll be waiting a long time for a powerful mood to strike, and second because it's more effective to oxygenate a small spark into a three-foot flame. Look for subtle effects, subdued responses, and understated feelings. Like a certain male body part, arousal starts out flaccid, but with a little massaging, it can grow to impressive lengths.

Remember the Time When...?

Once you identify the cues that make your body sit up, point, and yell "*Squirrel!*" it's important that you access your sexual memory bank. Specifically, for memories of the best sex you ever had. When was the last time a man kept you in the bedroom so long your family put your face on a milk carton? Play it back in the theater of your mind with a 70 mm camera and an IMAX screen. Where were you? What were you wearing? What were you doing? What was he doing? What were you feeling? What was he saying?

Basically, you want to add oxygen to the spark created by the cue. This is what I mean by desire being a decision. You *decide* to look for sexual cues. Then you *decide* to access them in a context where sexual response can flourish, and then you *decide* to fan it with flashbacks.

Cultivating sexual cues is like cultivating sensuality—by understanding what your body needs and freely offering it, the body pays you back with a higher mood state. Over time, you will gradually experience an increase in your sex drive. As you do, it'll be time for...

"Flicker Stage" Sex

Remember the days when your loins caught fire anytime your partner walked by? Forget about them—they're getting in the way. See, you're waiting for a dramatic, overwhelming sense of desire before having sex. High-libido people report dramatic stirrings in their stomachs (among other places) when they get sexually excited, while low-libido people don't. It's easy to act on your urges when you get physiological triggers that demand a response. But sexual signals in low-libido women aren't always that overt. Typically, low-libido women don't get excited *until* they have sex. Even when they do feel sexual stirrings, they're more likely to feel burning coals than raging fires. Start paying attention to subtle feelings and act on them. Wait. Did you just notice your partner's cologne when he walked by? *Don't keep reading this book; put it down and go kiss him.* Don't wait for the fire; act on the flicker. Ask any fireman—a spark is all you need to turn wood into a spectacle.

Sometimes of course, you don't even get a flicker to act on. In those cases you have to be willing to...

Have Sex Even When You Don't Feel Like It

I'm not talking about having sex to alleviate the guilt you may feel about withdrawing from your partner. Or doing it because you want to avoid more conflict. Or because you want to "take one for the team." Those are actually noble goals, but they're not ours.

Our goal is for you to understand that it's possible to start out not wanting it and end up not getting enough; to experience turning zero arousal into 60 mph sex. To understand that great sex doesn't always have to start with great desire. *The sex itself creates desire.*

Almost every woman has experienced a time when she didn't feel like having sex, "gave in" to their partner, and ended up having the time of their lives. Having sex when you're not aroused is like eating food when you're not hungry. Sometimes a sniff of the hot dog makes you want to put the whole thing in your mouth.

With relish.

Now, let's not be stupid here. You have the right to refuse sex anytime you want. This isn't about giving up control of your body. It isn't about forcing yourself to do something you don't want to do; it's about letting yourself do something that can take you to a better place. It's about experimenting with the idea that sex can create desire.

Now, there are certain things that will facilitate your willingness to have sex when you don't feel like it. Number one is teaching your partner what makes you hotter than lava. This is where all the work you did in Chapter Six comes in. You need to communicate everything you learned in your self-exploration. What specific things can he do to make the journey more pleasurable? Soft, petal-like kisses that grow stronger bit by bit? Where does he start? Behind your ears? How? Do you prefer a massage? Where? He's got to pay attention to what makes you wanna/gonna and do it well. This, of course, can be problematic, as men often think foreplay means shutting their eyes and bracing for impact. He's got to become your idea of a great lover, not his. The only way he'll become that is to tell him how you want your vagina vajazzled. Just remember that while training your guy to deliver what you like is helpful, in the end, your libido, like your orgasm, is yours to manage.

As you experiment with having sex when you don't feel like it, you will have initial thoughts like, "When will this be over? How long is this going to last? I forgot to call Mom." That's fine and to be expected. But in between these thoughts I want you to ask yourself, *How can I make this feel better? What can I do that will turn me on more?* They're the same questions you asked yourself in the cultivating sensuality chapter: *How can I get more physical pleasure out of what I'm doing? How can I make my body feel better? How can I enhance the physical sensations I'm experiencing?*

These questions are critical to your success (defined as moving yourself away from "I don't feel like doing this" to "I don't want this to stop"). But they are only half the equation. For what good is asking yourself a question you don't intend to answer? So, when you ask *How can I enhance the physical sensations I'm experiencing?* it is not a rhetorical question. Answer it. And follow up with action. If the answer is getting on top, get on top. If the answer is guiding his hand to the area below your clitoris rather than the clitoris itself, guide his hand. Deciding on desire isn't about making yourself feel desire, it's about taking actions that lead to desire.

Don't Know What Arouses You?

Make it up. Give yourself a pretend answer. You'll be amazed at how accurate you'll be. Pretending gives honesty permission to come out and play. If that doesn't help, try "what iffing" it. For example, you could say, "I don't know what would make this better, but what if I asked him to hold me in a way that makes me feel safer and protected?" Or "I don't know what would help me feel more, but what if I moved my pelvis more rhythmically?" Or think about a woman you consider sexy and ask yourself, "What would she ask for?"

Remember, our experiment isn't to get you to endure a lovemaking session. It isn't to white-knuckle your way until his climax.

It's to discover that you have the power to go from cold to hot by *making decisions* that lead to the heat.

How to Say "No" without Scarring Him for Life

You have the right to say no to sex anytime you want, and he has the obligation to respect that. But you have an obligation, too, and that's to make sure you don't reject him cruelly. You can make it easier on him by following my two golden rules of sexual rejection:

1. **Be affectionate.** Most "low desire" partners withhold affection, thinking it's the best way to head off an advance or to emphasize the point that no means no. Being cold and distant is an effective way of warding off sex, but at what price? There's a better way. Decline with affection. Guys can take rejection if you make them feel sexually desirable. If you hold him in a way that makes him feel wanted, if you touch him in a way that makes him feel like he's not the reason for your lack of interest, if you kiss him in a way that makes him feel physically attractive, if you act as if you're still in love with him, *if you wrap affection around your refusal*, you will get what you want without damaging the relationship.
2. **Postpone, don't reject.** Never say no without saying when. A postponement is easier to take than a rejection. Now, the trick here is keeping your word. You can't expect him to respect your boundaries when you break your promises.

As for your partner, he needs to spend a little more time in the Masturbatorium. Sometimes true love requires self-service. He also needs to learn how to handle disappointment. Just like you need to sometimes have sex when you don't want it, he needs to sometimes keep it zipped when he does. After all, you're in this thing together. A one-person sacrifice is like a hatchet—you'll just end up wanting to bury it in your partner's back.

Surprise Him by Initiating Sex

I know what you're thinking: *What!! Isn't it enough that I'm willing to have sex when I don't feel like it? I have to initiate it, too?* Actually, you do. Our goal isn't to respond to desire (anybody can do that); it's to *decide* on it. And what better way to practice your decision-making powers than to plan, prepare, and initiate sex? All on your terms, of course. Initiating sex not only forces you to think about what you need to make it enjoyable, but also to get in the habit of giving it to yourself.

Think of it as throwing yourself a party when you're not in a good mood. What would you do to make sure you had a good time? What type of music would you play? What kind of drinks would you pour? What type of food would you serve?

It's the same concept with initiating sex when your libido is low. What do you need to do to make it enjoyable? First on your agenda is understanding *when* your body best responds to sex. Early in the morning? Late at night? Dusk? Plan around it. What sexual cues can you activate? What moisture-making memories of past sexual encounters will help you look forward to it? And once the action starts, always remember what questions to ask yourself: *How can I get more physical pleasure out of what I'm doing? How can I make my body feel better? How can I enhance the physical sensations I'm experiencing?*

Initiating sex when you're not aroused is like agreeing to your partner's advances when you're not aroused. It's the same boat with a different captain. Either way, it's worth remembering that sex when you're not horny is like eating when you're not hungry. You force yourself to eat a few potato chips and the next thing you know you've poked a hole in the bottom of the bag and find yourself putting the gas station clerk in a headlock because he ran out of chips.

Try to initiate sex every seven to ten days. Do it as an experiment for you and a gift for him (he'll see it for what it is—a gesture of love that rescues him from the spiral of rejection he can't seem to get himself out of). By experiencing the power of calling forth desire, you'll go from being a low-libido victim to a low-desire victor. And in the process you may be surprised that your partner suddenly starts doing things you've been nagging him about. Gestures of love tend to bring out the best in everyone.

The Single Best Way to Lift Your Libido

Would you do a twenty-minute workout if you knew it would it dramatically improve your sexual desire? Break out your gym clothes, because some breakthrough studies have shown that an exercise I call "20/70" makes women locked, cocked, and ready to rock.

There are stunning new developments in our understanding of how exercise affects female sexual functioning. The findings directly contradict the scientific assumptions of the last forty years and may offer a radically different treatment protocol for women with low sexual desire.

This promising revolution started when a team of researchers led by Dr. Cindy Meston at the University of Texas at Austin discovered, almost by accident, that a specific type of exercise can significantly increase sexual desire even in women with low libido.

For the last forty years, clinicians, researchers, and theorists assumed that the parasympathetic nervous system, which governs erectile response in men, was also responsible for sexual response in women. There was no real empirical evidence for it. They just had no reason to think otherwise. Thus treatment of sexual dysfunction centered around activating the parasympathetic nervous system. For example, anxiety-reduction techniques (breathing, progressive muscle relaxations) activate the parasympathetic while inhibiting the sympathetic nervous system. They facilitate sexual response by decreasing negative thoughts that divert the processing and experiencing of erotic cues, but these techniques do nothing to stimulate arousal.

Dr. Meston questioned the basic if-it's-true-for-men-it's-true-for-women assumption and asked a startling question: Could the sympathetic nervous system actually be the mechanism that triggers sexual response in women?

Both systems work in complementary ways to keep the body running properly. For example, the parasympathetic nervous system contracts the urinary bladder while the sympathetic nervous system relaxes it. Sympathetic is responsible for excitement; parasympathetic for relaxation. Sympathetic accelerates the human body while parasympathetic decelerates it. These are important distinctions in the study of sexuality because treatment protocols that activate one system inhibit the other.

What Dr. Meston needed to test her hypothesis was something that would activate the sympathetic nervous system. She chose exercise, which in moderate-to-high intensities generates the amount of sympathetic nervous system activity necessary for testing. So here's what Dr. Meston's team did: They outfitted test subjects with a vaginal photoplethysmograph (VPG), a tampon-shaped device that illuminates the capillary bed of the vaginal wall and the blood circulating within it. As the amount of blood in the vaginal tissue increases, more light is reflected into the device. VPG is widely used to measure genital sexual arousal.

Test subjects were divided into an exercise and no-exercise group. The exercise group spent twenty minutes on a stationary bike pedaling at 70 percent of their maximum heart rate. Both groups were then shown an erotic film. As you'd expect, both the exercise and non-exercise groups experienced an increase in sexual arousal during the film, characterized by increased genital blood flow, clitoral erection, and increased lubrication. But it was in the exercise group that the VPGs lit up like Christmas trees. The women who exercised had significantly, sometimes dramatically, higher levels of sexual arousal than women who did not, even though they watched the same erotic film.

Now, the natural inclination is to conclude that exercise *causes* sexual arousal. Not true. Exercise sets the stage for it. Without an erotic stimulus there is no sexual arousal.

Here's the fascinating part. Exercise, *without viewing the erotic film*, lit up the VPGs, signaling significant changes in genital blood flow. But when test subjects were asked if they felt sexually aroused the answer was no. Dr. Meston noted that exercise can *physiologically prepare* your body for sexual activity, but you still need an erotic stimulus, a psychological cue that activates the subjective experience of arousal. In other words, exercise sets the table, but erotic stimuli serve the food.

What makes this study especially significant is that it's been replicated over and over with the same results across different groups of women, even with women taking antidepressants. Especially notable is a study on women who struggled with low libido. That study represented the first empirical evidence that women with low libido can be sexually aroused through activation of the sympathetic nervous system.

Again, it's easy to misinterpret these studies and think that exercise increases sexual arousal. It does not. Exercise followed by an erotic stimulus creates arousal.

Many of Dr. Meston's fellow scientists believe these studies herald a revolution in the treatment of low libido in women. For decades, the prevailing assumption was that the sympathetic nervous system *inhibited* sexual arousal in women. But now there is strong evidence to the contrary.

How Exercise Gets Your Body Ready for Sex

We know what exercise does to improve your sex life—it increases blood flow, which improves sensation, lubrication, arousal, and the intensity of orgasm. But exactly how does exercise do that? By strengthening the most important muscle in your body—the heart. Exercise, especially aerobic exercise (anything that elevates the heart rate for a sustained period of time—running, swimming, aerobics, etc.), builds a bigger, stronger heart that can forcefully pump blood and make it circulate faster through the body, including the pelvic region where increased blood flow is critical to arousal. Increased circulation means faster delivery of oxygen and nutrients to the body while speeding up the exit of waste and toxins.

Over time, the walls of the heart grow thicker and stronger, allowing it to pump more blood with less effort. It also increases the number and size of blood vessels in the tissues (including the vaginal walls), thus increasing the blood supply to all parts of the body.

Studies have also shown that exercise is the clitoris's best friend. Using clitoral color Doppler ultrasound (a technician presses a small handheld device, about the size of a bar of soap, against the clitoris), researchers at Fatih University, Ankara, Turkey, were able to prove that women who exercise had better clitoral blood flow than women who didn't. During sex, the clitoris increases in length and diameter because blood flow almost doubles during stimulation. Exercise facilitates the doubling. As an aside, if you're wondering why the clitoris, which is built with the same erectile tissue as the penis, doesn't get a rigid erection, it's because unlike the penis, there is no mechanism to trap the blood.

In addition to increasing blood flow (and activating the sympathetic nervous system), exercise has been shown to affect a variety of hormones linked with female sexual arousal—testosterone, cortisol, estrogen, prolactin, and oxytocin.

Exercise isn't a "good idea" for improving sex; *it is the single best thing you can do for it.* Without exercise you are endangering the restoration of your love life.

Putting the 20/70 Workout to Work for You

Simply having sex after you finish the 20/70 workout isn't going to help. You need to prepare an erotic stimulus after the exercise, which will then make you more receptive to sex. Remember, exercise does not cause sexual arousal, it sets the stage for it. It's the wood in the fireplace waiting for a light. The instrument for ignition doesn't matter. Erotic stimuli is defined as anything that makes you weak at the knees. It could be a film, a book, a poem, a memory, a picture, or anything else that would light your VPG.

Capitalizing on the 20/70 discovery requires a bit of planning: Schedule a romantic interlude with your partner ahead of time, pick your "erotic stimuli," do the 20/70 workout, take a quick shower, spend time with the erotic stimuli, and let the games begin.

The type of exercise you do (stationary bike, running, swimming) is irrelevant as long as it produces high levels of activation in the sympathetic nervous system. The studies defined high level as twenty minutes of sustained exercise at 70 percent of your maximum heart rate. To put the level of exertion in perspective, you should be able to carry on a conversation during the exercise. It's a 7 on the 1–10 scale of difficulty. Still, always consult your doctor before starting any new exercise regimen.

The real challenge isn't the exertion (it's moderately easy to do—test subjects were healthy, but not necessarily fit) but making sure that you stay within 70 percent of your heart rate capacity. The studies suggested that anything significantly below it doesn't produce enough sympathetic nervous system activity, and anything significantly above it may actually inhibit sexual arousal.

The easiest way to determine whether you're staying within your 70 percent capacity during exercise is to buy a heart monitor.

Costs have come down considerably—you can buy them for $50 to $100.

If you don't want to spend the money, you can make your own calculations with an age-predicted maximum heart rate formula by the American Heart Association:

226 minus your age = maximum heart rate x 70% = target heart rate (beats per minute)

Example for a thirty-year-old woman:

226-30 = 196 x .70 = 137

If you're thirty years old, your heart should beat at 137 beats per minute throughout the exercise. Make sure you maintain the pace by checking your pulse regularly during the exercise. You can feel your pulse by placing your fingers lightly but firmly over the inside of your wrist or on your neck just below the angle of your jaw. Count for ten seconds using your watch and then multiply by six.

Sex after a Workout?

Understandably, making love immediately after exercising isn't a particularly pleasant thought to many women. If you work out at a gym, where are you going to do it—in the locker room? In the car? Smelling like a petting zoo? Obviously, working out at home is advantageous. But what if you prefer—or need—to use the gym? Will the time it takes to get home, shower, and prepare decrease the 20/70's effectiveness?

The studies tested the presentation of the erotic film at five-, fifteen-, and thirty-minute intervals after the exercise ended. The results held for the fifteen- and thirty-minute intervals. The big question, unanswered by the studies, is how long the sympathetic nervous system activity stays high enough to set the stage for sexual arousal. No one knows, thus the call to study the treatment implications. But it stands to reason that if you're going to try this route, you should plan a lovemaking session as close to the end of the exercise as you can. *Without rushing yourself.* Putting pressure on yourself will neutralize the physiologic effect of the exercise.

Experimenting with the 20/70

The 20/70 studies are so promising that they justify experimenting with their findings, even if they cause some inconvenience. At the very least, you should consider a few self-pleasuring sessions after getting back home from a 20/70 workout. Always make sure to preplan your erotic stimuli—a video, a book, an engaging fantasy—anything that makes you, ahem, blink faster than normal. Remember, exercise does not cause sexual arousal—it accelerates it in the presence of a turn-on.

Incorporating the results of these studies into your sex life doesn't mean that you have to do the 20/70 every day or that you should only have sex after you exercise. The thing about exercising is that the more you do it, the better your blood flow will become, strengthening not only your libido, but also your ability to *feel* more. Exercise has been proven to rejuvenate nerve endings that heighten sensitivity to touch, all the while revving up your hormones.

The great news is that you don't have to exercise for very long to get the benefits. The 20/70 workout takes twenty minutes. That's less time than watching a sitcom. Hell, you've waited in line longer than that!

If 20/70 seems daunting, work up to it over the course of a month by starting with a "5/50 workout" —five minutes at 50 percent of your heart rate—and gradually increase the time and the intensity.

You don't have to exercise so hard that you crawl home into a fetal position every night to get the benefits. In fact, there's a growing body of evidence that exercising too much is detrimental to your sex life. For example, studies show that moderate exercise increases circulating androgens (sex hormones like testosterone, androstadienone, and dehydroepiandrosterone), but intense exercise *decreases* them.

My guess is that you don't like exercising, in great part, because you pushed yourself too hard for too long. Well, now you know you don't have to. But the bigger reason for your resistance might just be because you've been exercising for all the wrong reasons. Despite everything you hear to the contrary...

You Shouldn't Exercise to Lose Weight

Weight loss is the single worst motivation for exercise. It virtually guarantees that you will come to hate it and that you will eventually stop. To understand why, let's examine a peculiar contradiction. On the one hand, researchers have known for years that women who exercise have a better body image than women who don't. That's because exercise provides the basic building blocks of body confidence: competence, agency, and mastery. As you get faster, stronger, and learn new skills, you get a renewed sense of wonder and admiration of what your body is capable of doing. In fact, studies show that even between women of similar weight and shape, the women who exercise feel a lot better about their bodies than women who don't.

On the other hand, researchers noticed something unusual and unexpected: for many women, exercise *worsened* their body image. When they dug a little deeper, researchers discovered that exercise's effect on body image depends on your motivation for doing it. If you exercise to stay healthy and fit, your body image will most likely improve. If you exercise to lose weight, it most likely won't. Since many women have unachievable supermodel-weight-loss goals, they are bound to fail. Exercise as a tool for weight loss reminds them of how dissatisfied they are with their bodies. In fact, it creates more dissatisfaction because exercise as a weight-loss tool sucks you into that cycle of self-loathing we talked about earlier: Try, fail, shame. Try, fail, guilt. Try, fail, despair.

Exercising for the Right Reasons

Now, it's ridiculous to think that weight control won't be part of your motivation for exercise. Of course it will. But instead of seeing weight loss as a primary goal, see it as secondary consequence. Otherwise, exercise goes from being a stress-buster to a stress-maker.

So, before deciding on an exercise regimen, get clear on your motivation. You can easily tell if weight loss is your primary goal if you say things like, "Well, I'm going to have to hit the gym extra hard tomorrow" after eating a rich meal. The proper response to eating a rich meal is to enjoy it, not to punish yourself with exercise.

The primary benefit to exercise is health and fitness, not weight loss. Yes, exercise produces weight loss, but that is a by-product, not its purpose. You should work out to maintain optimal health, to reduce stress, anxiety, and depression. You should work out to get a sense of accomplishment, for a higher quality of life, for *fun*, to gain mastery and confidence, to build muscle, to increase energy levels, to strengthen your heart, improve circulation, prevent back pain, strengthen bones, improve posture, strengthen tissue around the joints, decrease risk for disease, improve mental functioning, increase confidence and self-esteem, improve sleep, increase resistance to fatigue, and reduce blood pressure.

In short, *you should exercise to promote an overall sense of well-being.* Which, as you know, promotes good sex, which promotes well-being. Exercise pops you into this powerful reinforcement cycle.

What If You Hate Exercise, *Period*?

Although the 20/70 workout doesn't require a high level of fitness, the idea of a moderate-to-intense twenty-minute workout can feel a little daunting to the committed couch potato. But then, *any* exercise is probably unappealing. Sofa spuds, I ask you to push the pause button on your resistance long enough to hear why exercise is so important to your sexual health.

It's worth remembering that there is only one thing more powerful than body image in determining women's sexual functioning—an overall sense of well-being. Recall the reinforcement cycle—well-being produces good sex, which contributes to well-being. Exercise inserts you into this reinforcement cycle by reducing stress, depression, and anxiety and by increasing blood flow to the genitals. It is the single fastest way to affect the psychology of well-being and the physiology of sexual arousal *at the same time*. It is so critical to your success that it behooves you to commit to an exercise plan that you can stick to, no matter what level of effort you exert.

The Couch Potato's Guide to Creating a Sex Exercise Regimen

The only exercise that matters is the exercise you're willing to do. So, this guide isn't so much about picking an exercise and showing you how to perform it, but about *forming an exercise habit*. Discipline and willpower will only take you through the first few weeks of an exercise program. Habit, on the other hand, is forever.

Pick an exercise you like or feel neutral about

No amount of motivation is going to overcome resistance to a hated exercise. Pick something you like, or at the very least, something you don't dislike. Never associate a habit with pain, only with pleasure. If it's at all possible, pick an exercise you can do outdoors. Some studies suggest that outdoor exercise can be as effective as antidepressants in treating mild to moderate depression and anxiety.

Vary the exercises frequently

Familiarity breeds contempt. Doing the same exercise day after day is a recipe for resignation. If you run on Monday, go to the gym on

Tuesday, swim on Wednesday, do aerobics on Thursday. Variety is a prophylactic to quitting.

Start slow

Don't exercise for an hour. Don't even do twenty minutes. Start with five minutes the first few days, adding thirty seconds every day until you get to ten minutes. Then use the same scale to get to fifteen and twenty minutes. Pain doesn't build habits; pleasure does. If you don't feel good after exercising, back off, you're doing too much. Success starts with the lowest intensity possible and gradually moves up.

Exercise every day for thirty days

Habits need daily reinforcement. You don't get in the cigarette habit by smoking twice a week. You don't get in the coffee habit by drinking it every few days. The only way to create an exercise habit is to condition it deeply enough to switch the behavior to autopilot. The best way to do that is to set a thirty-day challenge. Exercise every day, preferably at the same time. The more consistent the action, the more likely it will turn into a habit.

Create an exercise trigger

The latest science in habit formation shows that almost all habits have an event trigger. For example, having an alcoholic drink is a trigger for many smokers to pull out a cigarette. A shower might be a trigger for you to brush your teeth. Triggers work subconsciously to condition a behavior. The dinner bell rings and Pavlov's dog salivates. A morning exercise trigger might be a cup of coffee. Drink it and immediately grab your exercise gear and head out the door. Do it consciously for a sustained period of time and your subconscious will take over—you won't have to think about picking up your gym bag after you finish your cup. Triggers, like habits, take time to form. Do it every day if you want it to stick.

Set a consistent time

An event trigger isn't going to do you much good if you exercise at different times. Are you more likely to follow through in the mornings, at lunch, or in the evening? Set a consistent time and follow it.

Measure your progress

Seeing your progress will motivate to keep you going, enhance your body image, and increase the chance for success. Log your progress right away, as soon as you're done working out. Don't put it off. Don't make it complicated—just the date and what you did. Over time you're going to be amazed at your progress. When you go from five minutes of exercise a day to twenty, for example, a real sense of pride and accomplishment takes over.

Report to other people

Talk up your exercise to family, friends, and coworkers. Peer pressure helps form habits.

Reduce friction

If you wake up at five a.m. only to realize you can't find your sneakers, you might decide to go back to bed. Habit experts call obstacles like this "friction." They make habits more difficult to take hold. So, get your gear ready before bed so you can zoom out of the house without thinking about it.

Movement is medicine

There is one last benefit of exercise I haven't mentioned. It doesn't just set the stage for you to feel desire; it also makes you feel more desirable. One study found that women who exercised two to three times a week felt more sexually desirable than women who didn't. Move. Be active. Exercise. Your sex life is worth it. Your well-being is worth it. *You* are worth it.

Why Working Out with Your Partner May Sexually Arouse You

Neuroscientists at the University California at Berkeley recently made a breakthrough discovery: Sniffing a compound of male sweat called androstadienone causes hormonal, physiological, and psychological changes in women that result in sexual arousal.

Sweat has been the main focus of research on human pheromones. For example, we've known for years that male underarm sweat improves women's moods and affects their secretion of luteinizing hormone, which helps stimulate ovulation. Androstadienone is a derivative of testosterone that is found in all body secretions, but it is in especially high concentrations in male sweat.

In the most recent trials, women were asked to take twenty sniffs from a bottle containing androstadienone. Don't worry, they didn't gag. It smelled vaguely of musk. When compared to sniffing a control odor (yeast), the women who sniffed androstadienone reported significantly higher sexual arousal. Researchers also noted an increased physiological response, including blood pressure, heart rate, and breathing. These results were consistent with previous studies, but they also discovered a tantalizing new development—androstadienone has the power to elevate hormone levels. In this case cortisol, which is associated with alertness and stress. In fact, it remained elevated for a full hour after the sniff test.

So what does all this mean for you? The treatment applications for this discovery are unclear, but it will not hurt for you to work out with your partner and be conscious of sniffing his armpits (I suggest you do it when nobody's watching). Don't sniff when the smell is so bad it could peel the skin off a battleship. Do it when it smells good. Sweat is naturally odorless. It only begins to smell when bacteria that live on the skin digest sweat and excrete waste. That's why sweat smells clean in the beginning and slowly turns into mustard gas. By the way, he doesn't have to sweat enough to water a lawn; even a dab will do. Be sure to sniff his armpits when you're making out, having foreplay, or making love. The research is solid and beyond question: androstadienone changes mood and increases both sexual arousal (blood flow, lubrication) and physiological arousal (blood pressure, heartbeat). This doesn't mean taking a few sniffs of his pits will make your ankles float to the ceiling. They won't make you yell, "Take me like a vitamin!" The effects are far more subtle. What it does mean is that you have one more proven way to arouse yourself, and that, in combination with everything else we've talked about, will increase your libido.

Time to Decide

Over time, body consciousness can flatten desire like a recycled can. When sex becomes a reminder of your perceived deficits, your subconscious often lowers your libido to avoid the source of shame.

Body anxiety can also lower your ability to experience pleasurable sensations. Disruptive thoughts can put an oven mitt over nerve receptors, decreasing your ability to fully experience sensations or even recognize erotic cues.

Psychological, physiological, and contextual factors work in concert to create the desire for sex. It isn't one technique or the other that spells success. And it certainly isn't one at the expense of the other, either. For example, increased blood flow to the genitals will help but not if you're stressed, fatigued, or distracted. At the same time, being relaxed, focused, and willing won't work without enough blood flow. There are few black-and-white answers to sexual arousal, but there are lots of colorful contributions. Exercise is at the head of the list because it accelerates arousal (in the presence of erotic stimuli), maintains it through resolution, and builds capacity for it in the future.

Raising your libido can seem like raising the *Titanic*—an exciting proposition undermined by a lack of manpower, knowledge, and equipment. But *decisions* led the search party to find the *Titanic* and the right *decisions* will raise it off the sea floor. It's the same with your sunken libido. *Decisions* will raise it. By *deciding* to strike into the mood instead of waiting for the mood to strike, by *deciding* to capitalize on a spark with "flicker stage" sex, by *deciding* to exercise, by *deciding* to initiate sex, by *deciding* to use sexual cues, by *deciding* to ask yourself questions like, "How can I make this more physically arousing for me?" during lovemaking, you will discover just how much power you have to create a sex life worthy of your relationship.

How to Unplug Your Thoughts and Resurrect Your Love Life

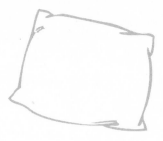

Let's review: You've gained some insight into why there's so much mental static in the bedroom. You now know that a better body isn't going to get rid of your appearance anxiety, that a lot of the women with bodies you idealize have terrible sex lives, that gorgeous women in the media actually give *men* appearance anxiety, that men actually prefer curvier women than you think they do, that when the men in your life say they're sexually attracted to you they mean it, and that when you're naked in bed men are enjoying, not judging your body.

You've also attracted and cultivated more sensuality into your daily life, so you understand how wonderful your body can feel and how ambiance (especially in the bedroom) can enhance or detract from tactile pleasure.

And hopefully you've been exercising, giving you a sense of control, accomplishment, and, more importantly, blood flow to the pelt beneath the belt. You've also learned how to create desire from thin air by identifying, cultivating, and acting on "cues" that trigger a sexual response, engaging in "flicker stage" sex, and training your guy to do things that make you hotter than July. You're almost ready to rock it!

In the next section I'm going to show you how to use sex to override all that appearance monitoring you do in bed. Note the word *override*. I'm not going to ask you to do visualizations, think positive, or convince yourself that you have a drop-dead body. None of that works. You can't out-think obsessive thoughts; you have to out-experience them.

Let's get you some experiences.

HOW TO TAKE YOUR
MIND OFF YOUR BODY
DURING SEX

"I'm so afraid my partner is going to lose his erection when he sees my body that I move around, cover up, or shut the lights so it won't happen. I play hide-and-seek because I feel like the penalty for being 'caught' is complete physical and emotional abandonment."

—Anna, 23, St. Louis, Mississippi

If I've done my job right, your body image hasn't improved a single bit. But you've experienced clarity about your faulty assumptions and you've learned a lot about sensuality, how your body works, and now that you're exercising and understand the power of contextual cues, you're kind of looking forward to a little hanky-panky.

But there's a problem. A big one. How can you be comfortable with sex if you're still obsessed with the "flaws" in your body? The answer won't make sense without first looking at how your anxiety gets expressed.

When Your Thoughts Get
More Action Than Your Body

There you are, making love to the man you love, and all you can think about is whether your thighs are jiggling. Sometimes, you actually feel like you've left your body and see it as an independent observer. It's called "spectatoring," the phenomenon of observing yourself as a third person in the bedroom. As a "spectator" in your own sex life, you inspect, monitor, and evaluate yourself to the point that you pay more attention to your judgments than to your partner or to what you're feeling. You're the referee throwing red flags all over the bed. Yes, he feels good inside you, but is he noticing that jiggle in your thighs? Because you notice it. And that's not all you notice. That faraway look in his eye? That's not pleasure. He's thinking of that new skinny girl from the gym! He wants to take you from behind? No way you're letting him see your back fat! He wants you to orgasm? But that means you'd have to stop holding your stomach in!

Intrusive thoughts during sexual activity are the hallmark of appearance anxiety. It's like you're not even thinking; you're being thought on. It's hard to let go and sexually respond to a partner when you feel like your body's on the auction block and the buyer is checking your hooves (among other things) to determine whether you're worth buying.

You worry that your partner shares your awful judgments and you brace yourself for the cutting comment, the disgusted look, and the suggestion of a trial separation. The anticipatory anxiety seizes you up. You're tense; you can't feel much except relief when he finally climaxes.

The pain and anguish of "spectatoring" can lead to pleasure-blocking behavior that reinforces your negative body image. You "cloak" your body in darkness or camouflage the objectionable parts with clothing. You try to block your partner from seeing objectionable parts of your body or position yourself in ways that he can't touch them. But mostly, you lie still because movement invites inspection.

Fortunately, there are several ways to get around "spectatoring" and the sacrifice of pleasure for judgment. It starts with a powerful tool that will teach your negative thoughts some manners.

The 25 Percent Factor

How do you measure the extent of a woman's body dissatisfaction? It's one thing to express dissatisfaction ("I hate my body"), quite another to measure it. One way researchers solved this dilemma was to conceptualize dissatisfaction as the discrepancy between perceived body size and true body size. This is commonly expressed as a "self-actual" discrepancy score.

This score is typically arrived at by measuring test subjects for BMI and then asking them to view an array of contour drawings, darkened silhouettes, or photographs of women's bodies arranged from thin to obese. The test subjects then circle the figure they feel best represents their true size and shape. The researchers then measure the discrepancy between the test subject's "actual" size and shape and their perception of it.

The results are as consistent as they are disconsolate: women *significantly* overstate the size and shape of their body.

Recently, a TV makeover show dramatized this type of "self-actual" discrepancy in live-action form. First, they take the measurements of eight or nine women of varying sizes and line them up in bras and panties, from thinnest to heaviest. The woman being "made over," herself in bra and panties, is asked to walk by the models, assess them, and then place herself where she feels she belongs in the lineup.

Inevitably, she places herself between two women who are much bigger than she is. The host moves her to the right spot—between two much thinner women. The contestant, of course, is usually shocked and ritually accuses the host of simply trying to make her feel better.

Women have a very skewed, inaccurate view of what their bodies look like. They over-estimate the size and shape of their bodies by as much as 25 percent or more. And by "they," of course, I mean you.

Twenty-five percent is a huge margin of error. The average 142-pound woman would have to gain 36 pounds to actually be 25 percent bigger. A woman wearing a size 12 would have to go up three dress sizes to be 25 percent heavier. A woman wearing a size 34 belt would have to wear a size 42 if she were 25 percent heavier.

How to Use the 25 Percent Margin of Error in Bed

Ladies, the woman walking in your mind is 25 percent heavier than the woman walking in your home. Those thighs? You may be right that they're jiggling, but you're wrong about how much. That stomach that's pooching out? You may be right, but your math is wrong. Back fat? Not even close.

We're going to use your inability to accurately gauge your shape and size as a powerful cudgel against your self-judgments. First, understand that there are three ways to have a relationship with a churning ocean. You can fight it (and drown). You can surrender to it (and drown). Or you can surf it (and live). We are going to use your 25 percent margin of error to surf the churning waves in your mind.

Every time you see a wave of negativity coming at you, use the 25 percent margin as a board and surf over it. Let's say you're in bed and it's getting hot and heavy with your partner. But all those intrusive waves of negativity keep crashing around you. Here's how you handle them:

Waves of Negative Thoughts	Your 25 Percent Surfboard
"My thighs are jiggling."	"Yeah, but they're jiggling at least 25 percent less than I think they are."
"My stomach is pooching out so much!"	"It's pooching out 25 percent less than I think it is."
"My hips are so wide!"	"They're 25 percent narrower than what I believe."
"My breasts are sagging!"	"I'm only 75 percent right."
[Insert your complaint here]	["It's not nearly as bad as I believe it is. If I were put in a lineup of similar-size women I'd be embarrassed to find out how much I overestimate the size of my body or how unappealing I think it looks."]

Think of It as a 25 Percent Discount off Your Judgments

You can't stop your negative thoughts, but you can take 25 percent off at the counter. No, it's not going to eliminate your body shame, but it will give you perspective. Enough to keep your negative thoughts in check so that your body can say "mate."

The wedge works because it's not trying to convince you that you have Miss Model's legs, Ms. Babe's butt, or Mrs. MILF's abs. It's giving you just enough wiggle room to go forward; it's taking off enough edge to keep you calm. You may not be able to countenance a big butt, but you can probably put up with a big butt minus 25 percent.

How much relief can a 25 percent margin buy you? Reducing your migraine by 25 percent still leaves you with a headache, but it's enough to get you to the office. Reducing your jet lag by 25 percent still leaves you groggy, but it's enough to let you sightsee. Reducing your anxiety by 25 percent still leaves you self-conscious, but it's enough to let you experience more pleasure.

The Secret to Turning Off Your Mind in Bed

The 25 percent margin factor gets you in the door, but a better approach to sex will keep you in the room. You don't realize it, but the way you're having sex can escalate your appearance anxiety. It's axiomatic in therapy circles that the attempt to solve a problem often exacerbates it, and my guess is that you are no exception to this rule.

Ladies and Gentlemen, I'd Like to Present...My Body!

From the time you were a little girl, you were conditioned to present yourself as a treasured object for visual inspection. Toddlers present themselves by twirling around in their new dress for Daddy. Little girls in leotards present their bodies at dance recitals. Teenage girls present their bodies at the beach. High school girls walk down the stairs and present their bodies to prom dates. Runway models present their bodies to fashion editors. Beauty pageant contestants present their bodies to judges. Brides present their bodies to grooms on the first night of their honeymoon. From pole dancers to porn stars, from swimsuit models to pool-side loungers, from college co-eds to TV anchors, every woman learns to present her body to a viewing audience.

You are conditioned to behave in a way that makes it easier for men to look at you. That's why, without being conscious of it, you approach sex with the characteristics that make it easier to be observed and judged: Being passive. Being still. Being silent. Submitting. Following instead of leading. Receiving instead of giving. Being acted upon instead of acting. It's much harder to conduct a visual inspection if the object being observed keeps moving, making distracting comments, creating diversionary energy, and not following your orders to turn around, bend over, and lean this way or that way so you can get a better look. There's a reason Miss America contestants don't move very much—it's harder for the judges to evaluate them.

But wait, you say! You don't *present* your body, you *hide* it. You cover it up, turn the lights off, and restrict yourself to sexual positions that conceal your body. Yes, but hiding requires you to use all the elements of an effective presentation: passivity, submissiveness, and silence. Hiding isn't the opposite of presenting; it's a form of it. Instead of presenting all of your body, you present some of it.

Being silent, still, and passive—requirements for hiding—seems logical to the body-conscious woman. After all, moving less, covering up more, and being quieter diverts attention away from your body, doesn't it? Yes. For him. *Not for you.*

Silence, stillness, and passivity force you to withdraw from activity. Withdrawing leaves you with *nothing else to focus on but your body.* And because there isn't, your attention cements to your appearance and multiplies your anxiety.

You're in a loop you can't get out of: silence, stillness, and passivity create more withdrawal, which channels your attention to your appearance, which feeds your anxiety. The anxiety prompts you to find better ways of covering and withdrawing, which further restricts your attention to your appearance. Pretty soon you expend so much energy and attention hiding and obsessing you can't be fully present for pleasure.

Withdrawing forces you to pay more attention to your body, not less.

The answer isn't to get a better body to present or find better ways to hide. It's to do the opposite of what you've been doing. The answer to presentation is participation. Be active instead of passive. Be communicative instead of silent. Be engaged instead of submissive. The secret to managing your mind in bed is to:

Be a vehicle for pleasure rather than an object to be looked at.

Be active. Talk. Move. Engage. Interact. Exchange. The more proactive you are in bed, the less reactive you'll be in your mind. It's hard to concentrate on any thought, let alone negative ones, when you're participating rather than withdrawing from an activity.

Move so you can stop being a sight to see and be a force to be felt.

From Presentation to Participation

Participation means getting involved and being engaged. It is contributing to an activity. Movement is the hallmark of activity because it creates energy. You don't have to haul out a trapeze or dance the Zoomba. You just need to move in a way that creates energy. Don't stay in a position for very long. Switch the way you kiss. Change the way you caress. Move right, fake left, run up the middle. Have sex Tivo style: Play...fast forward...slow motion... stop...rewind...play.

Get better in bed

Being active also means getting more out of giving pleasure than receiving it. That means learning how to give incomparable oral and unforgettable penetrative. Delight in making your partner's socks fly off his feet. In the next few chapters I'll show you tips and tricks guaranteed to keep you on the move, him on the edge, and your thoughts at bay.

Focus on your partner

You can't "not think" about your body. But you can think about another one—his. What turns you on about his body? His shoulders? His chest? His penis? Concentrate on those body parts and how they make you feel. Position yourself so you can better see and touch them. Explore his body as if it were a newfound treasure. Lose yourself in him. The more attention you pay to his body, the less attention you'll pay to yours. There's an old saying that you can't replace "A" with "not A." You've got to replace it with "B." You're "A." He's "B." Go see.

Start by paying attention to how he acts, what he says, how he breathes and the sounds he makes. Some women are shocked to find out that their partners are quite loud in bed. They've been so distracted by their internal dialogue of dissatisfaction that they didn't realize how expressive their partners were.

Focus on the physical exchange

Pay attention to stimulus and response. Oooh, if you stroke him there, he moans and kisses you harder. What would happen if you stroked him here instead? Wow, that tongue feels good inside you. What would happen if you moved a little to the left? Oh, that's perfect.

Talk

Compliment his body. Tell him what turns you on. Narrate the action. Whisper sweet nothings. Moan, groan, sigh. Talk dirty, talk back, talk sexy. Use your voice to get out of your head. You can learn the art of Tabasco Talk in a later chapter.

Focus on sensations

Use the skills you learned in cultivating sensuality. If you don't like your thighs, fine, but what do the satin sheets underneath them feel like? Don't like your stomach? That's okay. What does it feel like when he lies on top of you? Is his skin soft or rough? Is he hairy or smooth?

How to Stop Freaking Out about Being Touched

Almost every woman experiences a Defcon 5 moment when her partner touches, grazes, or, God forbid, holds a body part she doesn't like. It usually goes something like this: "Oh my god! He's touching my belly fat. He can *feel* how fat I am! Lord help me! *He's. Touching. My. Fat!*"

It can be an agonizing, catastrophic feeling—like he's going to lose his erection, roll off you, and turn the TV on to take his mind off Nightmare on Bed Street.

Just for the record, you're wrong. Men don't touch body parts they don't like. If he's touching your thighs or your belly, it's because he *likes* it. Male hands may be clumsy, but they are not dyslexic—they can see everything as it appears. They know exactly where they're going, what they're touching, and what they're holding. I know *you* may be freaking out that he's touching your belly, but *he's* not. Men touch women's parts because it turns them on.

Activate some double-duty rationality when he touches a forbidden zone. First, know we men move toward what we like and away from what we don't. Know this, and take it for what it is: your body is a turn-on to him. Of course, knowing that your partner didn't "accidentally" touch some perceived flaw—that he did it because he thinks it's lovely—can only reduce your panic so far. You can go further by putting the 25 percent factor into play. Consciously remind yourself that whatever he's touching is 25 percent smaller, tighter, and prettier than you give it credit for.

Still, an ounce of prevention is worth a pound of panic. I want you to try a powerful technique that will significantly reduce the panic you feel when he touches an objectionable part of your body. It comes courtesy of my girlfriend Cynthia, who taught me a valuable lesson about touching and being touched. She's a makeup artist who specializes in people who are facially disfigured by accidents and fires. As she talks about foundation and mascara with her clients, she does something completely unexpected—she puts down the eyeliner or whatever she's holding and touches their faces in a soft, loving way.

Her clients often weep, for it's the first time that anyone, let alone a stranger, touched their faces with such tenderness. "It's shocking enough that I touch them in an area they consider repulsive," says Cynthia, "but that I do it with love, without judgment or fear, is what makes it so emotional for them—and for me."

I think you should take my girlfriend's advice. Touch the parts of your body you don't want guys to touch and send love through your hands. Try a five-minute experiment right now. Close your eyes and put both your hands on your belly. Let the judgments come—it's not like you can stop them. After a minute or two you'll notice the judgment ease up a bit. Feel the heat from your hands and visualize an amber glow emanating from them and surrounding your belly. Say "I forgive you for not being flat and I forgive myself for placing such unrealistic demands on you." Send love through your hands the way Cynthia does for her clients. It is a moving experience that will transform the way you react to being touched in bed.

Managing Your Mind by Managing the Energy

Any activity that brings attention to your body is going to redline your body consciousness. Try walking past an attractive group of people in your bathing suit and see what happens. Sex, of course, is the mother of all anxiety-provoking activities. It requires you to disrobe in front of somebody who's going to pay careful attention to your body.

Often this immobilizes you. The more you move the more he sees, and you don't want that. So you discourage new positions, especially the ones that might highlight your perceived flaws. Pretty soon you're still as a statue and that's when you inadvertently create more of what you so spend so much energy avoiding—attention on your body. By withdrawing from sex you have nothing to focus on but your perceived flaws. That's why the first step out of this trap is to be active in bed. Remember:

Be a vehicle for pleasure rather than an object to be looked at.

Being a vehicle rather than an object means you can drive your attention away from self-judgments to better lands—like your partner's body, the sensations you create, and the ones you experience.

Move so you can stop being a sight to see and start being a force to be felt.

9

USING SEXUAL COMPETENCE TO BUILD BODY CONFIDENCE

"About the only time I can stop thinking about how my partner must be judging my body is when we're kissing. Maybe it's because his eyes are closed and he can't see me, but I think it's also because I know I'm a good kisser and it drives him insane when we make out. I feel powerful, knowing that I have that effect on him, and when that happens, I actually forget to be embarrassed by my body."

—Linda, 25, Chapel Hill, North Carolina

want to share a secret little known outside research circles. There's a specific type of woman who rarely experiences body consciousness during sexual activity. I'd like to paint a picture of this woman, as taken from the studies: She wears a size 2 dress. And 4, 8, 10, 12, 14, 18, and sometimes 20. She's in her twenties. And thirties, forties, and fifties. She's single. Though in many cases, married. Often as not, she has kids. She tends to be pretty, but then again, not really.

You see, she's every woman with one simple characteristic: she's good in bed.

Researchers discovered that competence is incompatible with self-consciousness. As Dr. Michael Wiederman noted in a 2000 *Journal of Sex Research* study:

> Women who viewed themselves as good sex partners were least concerned about their bodily appearance during physical intimacy, even when holding body size and body dissatisfaction constant.

It's the last phrase that makes the conclusion so powerful: "*even when holding body size and body dissatisfaction constant.*" In other words, you don't need to be satisfied with the way you look to stop body consciousness; you don't have to lose weight to end the cycle of shame in the bedroom. When you can value yourself for something other than how you look, your attention focuses away from judging your body and onto the value it brings to the table. Or the bedroom, as the case may be.

This is an incontrovertible fact in the building of positive self-image: Skill slackens self-hate. Capacity crowds out critiques. Competence trumps self-consciousness. Competence in bed—mastering the art of giving pleasure—quiets the beehive of your buzzing negativity.

The Secret to Being Good in Bed

Think back to the most memorable sex you've ever had. What do you remember most—that thing he did with his tongue or the feeling of getting sucked into a vortex of sexual energy that made you temporarily forget your name?

Being good in bed isn't just about technique. It isn't about what you can do to him; it's about where you can take him. It's not that technique isn't important; it's just that it's insufficient. Getting good at the mechanics makes you a skilled worker. Understanding how to shape passion into a give-and-receive union makes you a sublime lover. So before we dive into techniques, let's paddle around this passion thing.

Passion is a funny thing. You can't teach it because it's not a skill. You can't acquire it because it's not a possession. And you can't learn it because there are no instructions. Like the wind, you can't see it but you can feel it.

While you can't "teach" passion, you can learn how to set the stage for you to express it in your own unique way. If passion has one defining characteristic, it's energy. Movement. Action. Convergence.

By movement I don't mean sexual calisthenics—setting up a trapeze, swinging from the chandeliers, and diving into pillowed mosh pits. There's nothing wrong with that, but passion defines movement as something that builds and resolves anticipation. Movement that creates the unexpected. Movement that travels from dissonance to harmony. It can be subtle, silent, or loud. It can make you shiver, sigh, or scream. It can pull you down like a whirlpool, suck you up like a tornado, or waft you aloft on a magic carpet.

Consider the passionate kiss:

He stops an inch before your lips. The space between crackles with anticipation. He doesn't back up. He doesn't move forward. You're caught in his tease. Your heart climbs the stairs. He leans in. Your lips part and...

This is sexual energy in motion: It holds a chord and waits for the resolving note. It pushes you to the brink and pulls you back just in time to push you again. It has an upward trajectory, transferring from one partner to the other. Movement is passion's starting point. It can be subtle (an unresolved kiss) or explicit (throwing each other around like rag dolls).

Let's do an experiment. Think your worst thought about your body. Got it? Okay, now really concentrate on that thought as you follow my directions: Rub your hands together as fast as you can for ten seconds. Notice the tingling sensation when you stop?

That's movement creating energy, which manifests as heat. Now where did that awful thought of yours go? Poof! Movement creates energy that makes thoughts disappear.

Now, with passion as the backdrop, let's get back to skills. Being good in bed doesn't mean knowing every position in the Kama Sutra. It's combining sexual energy (movements characteristic of passion) with pleasure-giving skills. Remember, bedroom competence creates body confidence. Your goal is to get so good at sex that the laziest guy on earth would take one look at you and say, *"You make me want to get a job."*

Giving Unforgettable Oral

Can I tell you a secret about men? We are alarmingly overattached to our penises. In fact, we love listening to "He's Got the Whole World in His Hands" when we pee. You can make your partner feel like he's got the whole galaxy in his hands with the right kind of oral. Unfortunately, a lot of women agreed with Mink Stole when she delivered her classic line in John Waters' film, *Female Trouble*: "I wouldn't suck your lousy dick if I was suffocating and there was oxygen in your balls!" This is, to say the least, unhelpful. Typically, women have three major objections to giving oral—taste, smell, and discomfort—all of which are easy to, ahem, overcome. Throw your guy in the shower, find positions that don't choke you, and concentrate on what the penis represents—the essence of your partner's masculinity.

Even women who like (or don't mind) going down on a guy tend to give what a friend calls "Ukrainian blowjobs"—well-meaning, but dull. That might be because they don't know that giving great oral requires three things: moisture, speed, and friction. Success starts with saliva. The most natural way of generating it is to bite into a sour apple or suck on a hard candy. Notice how it makes you drool? It's your body's way of fighting off the acidity in the mouth (the saliva dilutes it). Of course, you don't want to bring apples into the bedroom, so try this instead: visualize biting into a lemon.

Your hand is the next most important thing. You need to deliver three things with it: friction, pressure, and speed.

Use your hand as an extension of your mouth. Do this: Make a fist and punch yourself in the chest. Your knuckles should be touching your chest, with your thumb facing toward you. That's your starting position. With your hand in that position, twist/stroke on the way down and stroke/twist on the way up. You're basically doing a corkscrew motion as you wet him with a constant stream of saliva. Your mouth may give him moisture and heat, but it doesn't give him pressure and friction. That's what the hand is for.

If you can get these basics down—moisture with your mouth, and speed, pressure, and friction with your hand—you're well on your way to mastery. Then it's a matter of add-ons, like pretending there's oxygen in his balls and making your attempts sound like half-price day at the liposuction center.

Remember, talent without passion makes you a skilled laborer. Think about why you love his penis, not just what you can do with it or to it. Is it the thrill of feeling him get hard in your mouth? The power to arouse him? The feeling of submission when you look up at his eyes? Its strength and hardness? The masculinity of its smell and feel? How it can dominate you? Is it the sheer novelty of seeing and feeling a part of him you don't ordinarily see? The anticipation of bathing it with your mouth before it's inserted into your body?

Without thinking about, acting on, and expressing these feelings, you're just going through the motions. Get in touch with why giving oral is pleasurable for *you*, and you'll be able to combine skill with passion to create a memorable experience. When it comes to sex, it's better to suck at something you love than to excel at something you don't.

Stake your position

It's hard to give pleasure when you're in pain. The most common position—your partner on his back with you kneeling between his legs—is unsustainable because it's so uncomfortable. The best positions are the ones that support you while giving access to a big part of your partner's body. For example, he's on his back to your left. You sit up and put your left arm over and across his belly (so your armpit is snug against his sides). Your back is to him but you have a grand view of his manhood. The weight of your lower body is being supported because you're lying down while your left arm anchors you. Or you can sit on the bed while he stands. Or prop up your pillows and lie back on them as if you were reading a book. Have him straddle you. Men love some version of this position because they like seeing things go in and out and in and out—and did I mention in and out?

The point isn't necessarily to give you an endless list of positions; it's to emphasize your comfort. You will never get good at any aspect of sex if you don't find a position where you're comfortable enough to do your best work.

Being playful with a mouthful

Giving oral can be active or receptive. Both have their joys, but being active is particularly useful to keep the self-judging hounds at bay. For example, sit on the edge of the bed with him standing in front of you so you're eye to eye with his third eye. Now practice the alphabet with your tongue. Do the easiest letters first: M and W. Start at the bottom of his right testicle, go up, trace an "M" on his crotch, and finish at his left testicle. Go from right to left, then from left to right, a few times. Then do the W. Always make sure to touch his body with your hands—stroke his inner thighs, the outer legs, his stomach, chest, and buttocks. Think of it as giving him a 360-degree sensurround experience.

An equally playful version is something called "paint the canvas." Pretend your tongue is the brush, his crotch is the canvas, and your saliva is the paint. First, you're Van Gogh—painting swirls around his testicle and inner thighs. Then you're Monet, putting wet pointy kisses all over his perineum, working your way up to his penis. Then you're...well, who's your favorite artist?

Master the basics and everything else comes together

These recommendations aren't meant to be a full catalog of the things you can do to be a better lover. We're covering the basics because if you don't get that right, nothing else matters. Remember, there's only one way to get good at something: practice. Once you feel more confident, you can add a little more creativity in the following ways:

Pressure point pleasures

You're kneeling between his legs. You spread his legs apart but with his knees bent toward his chest. You hold his penis in your wet mouth, bobbing gently while your hands find the middle of his hamstring muscles. Gently press one or two fingers into each hamstring. Move the pressure point to the left and right and press. Gently at first and then with increasing pressure (but never enough to hurt). In many men, activating a pressure point while receiving oral is a signature, unforgettable pleasure.

The sloppy diamond

Put your partner on his back at the edge of the bed where you can kneel and have access to his whole body. Picture a line drawn from his penis to his right nipple to his mouth to his left nipple and back to his penis. That's the diamond path your mouth will travel.

Start by sucking the head of his penis gently, maybe two or three bobs, then go to his right nipple and suck on it two or three times. Then go for his mouth and give him two or three very wet kisses. Following the diamond line, go to his left nipple and back to his cock.

What'll really make him grab the sheets is when you start varying how you go down the diamond path of his hot zones. For instance, going from his penis to his mouth back and forth, ignoring his nipples. The inability to predict builds anticipation. So be unpredictable. While you're traveling down the diamond path with your mouth, your hands are free to double his pleasure. You can, for example, put a left-hand finger in his mouth while stroking his balls with your right. While kissing him you could caress his face. While sucking on his nipples you could stroke his inner thighs. Either way he's going to go radioactive with pleasure.

The sloppy diamond is a great example of what I meant by participation in the last chapter. When you withdraw by being passive and still, there is nothing to pay attention to but your anxious thoughts. When you're engaged, active, moving, concentrating on your partner's body, building a skill, noticing reactions, and changing directions, the only thought you're going to pay attention to is your next move.

From Bada Bing to Bada BANG!

The single most important thing you can do during intercourse is to express your love for it. Intercourse is an exchange of energy, passion, and love. It is not a deposit from him to you; it's an exchange. It's not about what's inserted into you but what it brings out of you. Think of it as active reception. You are taking as much as you're giving. Nothing ruins a man's enjoyment more than a bored-looking woman lying still while he bangs away like a buck-toothed nanny goat. Do not look at the ceiling and wonder how it would look in beige. Your job as a good lover is to use movement and sound to amplify energy and passion.

Oooh, ahhh, huff, puff, gasp!

Be noisy. Scream, moan, talk, laugh (but not at him). There is no energy without movement. Go right, fake left, bend low, go up the middle. Get into it. Zing, zip, rest, start over. Not feeling it? Fake it. Not for him, for you. The more you lie still, the more you become an object to be looked at. And that, as you know, is the fear that drives you to avoid sex or put conditions on it. There is only one thing to do with a statue: visually inspect it. But there are many things to do with a woman who expresses her delight with movement. I'm not saying you should become a trampolining, cheerleading banshee in bed, but you do need to move and make sounds that feel right to you. If that's a problem, start with a low moan, a little wiggling, and work your way up. It isn't volume or the level of motion that counts: it's the depth of your physical involvement.

Connect with him in meaningful ways. You are not simply giving him your vagina: you are giving him his masculinity, his virility, his worth. Express this gift-giving joy in physical ways that are meaningful to you. Raise your hips to greet his thrusts, lift your pelvis to welcome his penis, put your emotional state on external speaker. *Expend energy.* There's love in the air. Breathe it in. And remember this always: Statues get stares. Movers get love.

The Three Most Important Factors That Make Intercourse Enjoyable for a Man

Wetter, hotter, tighter makes men harder, harder, harder. The pleasure of your vagina's lubrication, warmth, and fit will make him incapable of thought. Let's start with lubrication. Are your juices flowing? Some women can get wet at the thought of water; others can't seem to turn the faucet on. The propensity for self-lubrication varies from woman to woman. It is not true that a lack of adequate lubrication is a sign that you're not attracted to your partner or that there's something wrong with you.

If you can't get your wet on, check out a couple of possibilities. Start by looking at your medicine cabinet. Lots of medicines cause vaginal dryness. There are other factors, too—hormone levels, stress, diet, sleep, drugs, and lack of exercise. And, of course, being shut down about sex because you're obsessed about the way your body looks.

Estrogen is a major factor in vaginal self-lubrication. The more you have, the wetter you'll get. Estrogen levels fluctuate during the menstrual cycle, and that's why you'll notice different amounts of lubrication throughout the month. Unfortunately, there are no pills or medication (other than hormone replacement therapy) to help you produce more lubrication.

Still, there are a few things you can do to get your fountains working. Self-generated lubrication is a reaction to arousal. You may simply need more nonsexual touching, kissing, and fondling to get you going. Men are like rockets—all we need is a launching pad and we hit the heavens. Women, on the other hand, are more like airplanes. You need a long tarmac to make a gradual ascent. You get higher and stay aloft longer than men; you just don't get there as quickly. So give yourself a break—slow everything down and make foreplay last a little longer. That, of course, is more of a problem for him than it is for you. There's a reason men don't blink during foreplay—they don't have time. Still, you can slow down Speedy Gonzalez by guiding his hands and communicating your needs.

Next, masturbate more often. It primes the pump. Having sex regularly fuels and trains your body to self-lubricate more easily.

If all else fails, use a water-based lube. Use it well, use it often, but mostly, use a lot of it. When it comes to lube, nothing succeeds like excess. Your natural lubrication may not make it all the way up to your clitoris, so be sure to include the area.

I'm emphasizing lubrication because it drives men insane with pleasure. Your lubrication is his limousine to the asylum. Test time: Dry your lips completely and run a finger over them lightly. Now lick your lips and do it again. Which is more sensual? Wet sex is hot sex.

If wetter is better, then tighter is righter

How tight is tight? Well, you don't want your vagina putting his penis in a headlock, but at the same time, he should be able to feel you down the whole length of his penis. It should feel like a glove—snug but easy to get into. The best way to keep your vaginal glove tight and right is to exercise your pelvic floor muscles.

Studies show that weak and deconditioned muscles not only interfere with vaginal friction (the tight fit that men dream about), but also withhold blood flow to the area. In particular, a weak ischiocavernous muscle, which attaches to the clitoral hood, can depress genital arousal and inhibit orgasm. The good news is that studies show you can *greatly* improve vaginal elasticity, muscle tone, and blood flow through Kegel exercises, which contract and release the pelvic floor muscles.

First, find your pelvic floor muscles. They're the muscles you use to stop urinating. The basic exercises are the "flutter" (tighten and let go quickly) and the "pinch and hold" (tighten and don't let go till you count to fifteen; as you get better, hold it for longer). You need to work up to a couple hundred reps a day for a few weeks before you notice the effects. To get the best of your Kegel exercises, don't do them all while sitting or standing: try lying on your back or side or while squatting. Different positions help give your muscles better tone.

You'll know your vaginal walls are strengthening when his penis begins to feel thicker and larger inside of you. Now, clearly, once you get fully lubricated and excited you will loosen up. Use the "flutter" and "pinch and hold" exercises to give him an extra treat when he's inside you. It'll feel like you're giving his penis a massage.

Friction addiction

Keeping your vagina strong and supple allows you to create a delicate blend of pressure, friction, and tightness that will dilate his pupils as well as his penis. Think of your vagina as the personal masseur to his penis. Hold him deep inside with your muscles. Push him in provocatively. Push him out erotically. Contract. Release. Quickly. Slowly. Sensually.

Sexual Competence Builds Bedroom Confidence

Commit to competency. When you become a vehicle for pleasure, you stop being an object to be evaluated. By focusing on what your body can do rather than what it can look like, you bypass anxiety's awful, life-sucking energy.

Confidence is the wake left by competence. Women who are good lovers, women who are competent in bed, develop a sense of control and wisdom about their bodies. They're more confident about their bodies because their self-judgment now includes competence and mastery as well as appearance.

Low confidence and low competence tend to go together. The anxiety you have over what your body looks like will wither when you stop waiting for confidence and start building it with competence.

Remember, your goal isn't to feel good about your body. It's to feel good about what your body can do. The route to confidence is competence, not thinness. The ability to give a man pleasure changes the way he looks at you. He will be filled with gratitude, admiration, and respect for all of you, not just your body. He will feel more emotionally connected, spiritually bonded, and physically attracted to you. This ability to enhance the quality of your relationship—this *competence*—not only straps a rocket to the back of your confidence, but also dramatically improves your overall sense of well-being, which, as you know, is more important than body image in creating a fulfilling sex life.

10

TABASCO TALK VS. NEGATIVE TALK

"I'm a naturally talkative person but not in bed. As soon as we get naked, all I can think about is what my partner thinks of my body. The shame silences me."

—Barbara, 26, Tulsa, Oklahoma

Let's do a test: I want you to think about a part of your body you don't like while reading aloud this sexual passage in Toni Morrison's *Beloved*:

As soon as one strip of husk was down, the rest obeyed and the ear yielded up to him its shy rows, exposed at last. How loose the silk. How quick the jailed-up flavor ran free. No matter what all your teeth and wet fingers anticipated, there was no accounting for the way that simple joy could shake you. How loose the silk. How fine and loose and free.

It's hard to hold on to the negative thought, isn't it? Talking about one subject while thinking about another is like trying to have an interesting conversation while you're watching a repeat of a dreadful show—you're going to pay a lot more attention to the new dialogue than the old monologue. Erotic talk—verbalizing all aspects of your sexual experience—doesn't leave much space for your inner dialogue. Here's why: Talking is *participating*, and participating gives your obsessive mind something else to focus on other than your appearance.

Erotic talk isn't just a diversion from your thoughts, of course. Just like talking about a delicious meal can make it tastier, erotic talk can make sex more appetizing.

What Does Talking Sexy Mean?

Most people think "talking dirty" is a vulgar, in-your-face, prison-style accounting of what you want to do behind closed doors. But it's just as often a delicate, tender expression of your love. Talking erotically means different things in different contexts. It can deepen love or heighten lust. It can help you access sexual fantasies, express your emotional bond, or simply reveal all that is naughty within you. It can be an observation you make of your partner's body, a compliment of his lovemaking, a narrative of what's going on, a preview of coming attractions, an anticipatory exclamation, a sigh, a moan, or a cry. It's an expression of what you like, a communication of what you want, or an appreciation of what was delivered. It's the language of love and it can rise to the sky or descend to the gutter. It can be aggressive or tame, naughty or nice, instructive or illuminating. It is many things but it is always *expressive*.

Erotic talk starts before the clothes come off and doesn't end until you pull the sheets over you. As you can see below, sexy talk brightens every phase of the sexual experience:

Presex
"I love running my fingers through your hairy chest."
"You have amazing hands."
"I want to kiss every inch of you."

Foreplay

"I love watching your penis get hard."

"I love it when you do that."

"Do you like it when I touch myself here?"

Sex

"You taste so good I could do this forever."

"You feel so good sliding in and out of me."

"I love the sounds you make when you come."

Postsex

"That was amazing."

"Hold me closer, I want to absorb everything we just did."

"Have I told you lately how much I love you?"

Talking dirty doesn't have to be dirty. As you can see, there's a lot more to it than the lunatic ravings of a horny junkyard dog (although there is much to say for that, too). Learning the art of sexy talk is easy. All you have to do is...

Notice the sensations in your body. *Express them.*

Ask for what you want. *Talk about it.*

Anticipate how good it's going to feel. *Breathe heavy.*

Think about your fantasy. *Voice it.*

Notice his body. *Compliment him.*

Does it feel good? *Tell him.*

Do you like the way he's touching you? *Moan.*

Are you getting wet? *Groan.*

Are you close? *Announce it.*

Erotic talk is about reflecting, creating, or intensifying passion through sounds and words. It's caressing your lover with language. Erotic talk is an important part of rebuilding your sex life because...

Staying in the moment keeps you from staying in your judgments.

Staying present is a big challenge for body-conscious women. Seizures of self-judgment colonize your attention to the point that you can't be in the here and now. Talking is a powerful way of preventing your mind from wandering into toxic terrain because it forces you to stay in the moment. Besides, it makes sex fire on all five cylinders. Sex is terrific with taste, touch, sight, and smell, but talk brings it all together. A four-cylinder engine will take you where you want to go, but adding a fifth will get you there quicker and the ride will be more memorable.

Passionate sex is about creating and releasing energy. Talking is energy—in the form of noise vibrating in distinct patterns and pitches. You don't just hear sound, you feel it. There's scientific backing for this. Speaking or hearing sexually charged words is known to spike dopamine transmissions in brain chemistry, triggering sexual excitement.

Erotic talking is a release of pent-up energy. It gives voice to our innermost desires in ways that our bodies can't. It creates energy not just by the physical vibration or your emotional intent, but by prompting your partner to respond. Energy feeds on energy. Every word you say builds a step your partner climbs up on. And everything he says builds a step for you to rise. Keep climbing. Heat rises. Sometimes words get in the way, but other times they *pave* the way.

When You're Too Shy to Try

A lot of women find it hard to be verbally expressive in bed because, well, they don't think of themselves as that kind of girl. The fear of being branded a slut, of being judged for being so forward, for acting against your own self-image, or simply being scared of saying something truly lame is enough to treat the bedroom like a library, where even loud shirts are frowned upon. Whether you're a demure twentysomething, a sophisticated career woman, or a sweet-natured mother of two, talking dirty can seem off-target, like it's meant for another type of woman.

Of course, being self-conscious about your body adds another layer of reticence. Will talking sexy attract more unwanted attention? How do you express yourself erotically when you hardly want to be in bed in the first place? What if you're usually silent in bed? Exactly how should you proceed? Slowly. You can't go from somebody who never utters a peep to somebody who yells, "Drill me with that axis of evil between your legs!"

First, never say that. Second, if you're in a relationship with a guy who's so uptight he could crack nuts with his butt cheeks, it might be wise to let him know in advance that you want to talk sexy. Otherwise, you will define awkwardness for the next generation and provoke suspicion to boot. ("Where did she learn that kind of talk? Is she cheating on me?" "Where did she get that awful line?")

That said, most guys love Tabasco Talk. Why do you think they spend $3.99 a minute to hear it? You most likely don't have to warn him it's coming, especially if you start slowly and gradually work up to more earthy, lusty language.

The First Step to Becoming Bed-Lingual

Start by observing him. What words does he use? What sounds does he make? Does he sigh or moan? When? Is it loud or soft? What effect does it have on you? What words does he repeat? What's your reaction? Shock? Dismay? Arousal?

Pay attention. Notice. Observe. Then mirror his sounds. If he moans, moan with him. If he breathes hard, breathe hard with him. You're probably already doing this without knowing it. Romantic partners subconsciously mirror each other's body language.

If you truly don't make a sound in bed, following your partner's sounds will help, but keep in mind that there's a difference between mirroring and aping. If his moans are deep and guttural, make yours a little shallower and high-pitched. If his are long, make yours short. Mirroring ping-pongs the energy higher and higher. Aping just makes him feel like you're mocking him.

What if you're not feeling anything strongly enough to moan or groan? That isn't hard to imagine for body-conscious women because if you're suffering with low libido or low sensation then you might not feel anything too intensely. But you're most likely feeling *something* and you can certainly give verbal expression to that.

If you feel funny about moaning or groaning for a feeling that isn't there (or a feeling you don't think justifies a sound), do it anyway because the act of moaning or sighing can create the feeling or make it grow stronger. Just because you don't feel it doesn't mean you can't get yourself to. Remember, you may not be hungry but the smell of a good hot dog can make you put the whole thing in your mouth. A little acting, a little effort, and whoa! Where did that orgasm come from? Get comfortable with sounds, and you'll get comfortable with words. Once it's easy for you to sigh, purr, or cry out, you're ready for the next step.

Develop your own code words

If you've got a bad case of verbal performance anxiety or you're too afraid you're going to end up saying something ridiculous ("axis of evil!"), develop a code for words you find difficult to say. For example, you could say, "Can we do my favorite thing?" to indicate missionary style. "Tease me" could be a stand-in for oral sex. And "My turn" could stand for, well, your crack at whatever he was doing.

I want to verb your noun

It's not what you say but *that* you say. As you get more comfortable with making sounds and forming words during lovemaking, it's time to get a little more explicit. But first, let's practice. Find your favorite passages from the erotica that you've hopefully already gone out and bought. Read it out loud to yourself first so you can get the hang of it and won't feel so self-conscious when you're with your partner.

When you're ready to go solo, keep in mind that talking sexy is supposed to be fun. You're merely expressing your sexuality with words. If you think you've got to come up with something flowery, *stop*. Back up. Let me introduce you to the first rule of Tabasco Talk: *no poetry*. Any word with more than two syllables is a word with too many syllables.

A great way to ease into the process is to practice on the phone when you're out of town. Some women find it easier because there's no eye contact, and the distance provides an emotional buffer. Another good way to get comfortable with naughty words is to play a word game I call Naughtirati. Your partner draws naughty words on your naked back and you guess what they are. Be playful. This isn't serious. It's fun. And wet, too, if your partner draws the words with his tongue. Can you guess what he's writing? Louder, I can't hear you!

Okay, so we started with mirroring the sounds your partner makes in bed, then to developing code words, then to reading erotica passages out loud to yourself, then to guessing what naughty words your lover drew on your back. Now you're ready for....

The Erotic Appreciation Exercise

Simply notice something about his body that you like and say something about it ("I like the shape of your penis when it's completely hard"). Then say something about his style of lovemaking. Like, "I love the way your kisses automatically make my nipples erect." It's simple, really. Notice something you like about your partner *and tell him*. All you're doing is putting your thoughts on external speaker. If you feel a little awkward, try whispering it in his ear.

Narrate the action

The next step is to describe what's happening. Is he stroking your thighs? Then say something like, "I love the way you touch the inside of my leg." Do you want to go down on him? Then say, "I really want to go down on you." Describe what you're doing and feeling. Remember: it doesn't matter what you say, only that you say it.

Sensual listening

Your partner isn't exactly going to be silent when you start talking, and he deserves the same kind of openness and acceptance you'd like from him. Instead of trying to decide whether your partner's utterances are appropriate, silly, cliched, or offensive, judge them by their power to arouse you. This is important because words are aphrodisiacs, and if there's something that he says or the way he says it that turns you on, you need to respond positively so he knows to keep saying it in the future.

By the same token, if there's something that's offensive, you need to tell him that, too. I had a girlfriend who finally had the nerve to ask her boyfriend to talk dirty to her, and he ended up calling her a dirty whore every time they made love. Not exactly what she was hoping for. Remember the universal law of questions: If you want something, ask for it. If you want something stopped, ask for that, too.

What Not to Say in Bed

Desires shouldn't be demands. It's one thing to ask for something, another to make it sound like a requirement. If you want to cause a firm case of situational impotence, you can't do any better than saying things that sound like you want a command performance.

For example, if your partner has problems with premature ejaculation, telling him that you want to make love for hours on end is going to feel like a lot of pressure. Your words are meant to entice and provoke, not threaten.

Engage the Erotic Feedback Loop

Energy requires dialogue, not monologue. Amp it up by responding to the things he says or does. If he says, "I love putting it all inside you," you can say, "Me too, especially when you slide it in and out of me so slowly." Not only are you creating more energy, but you're also giving him erotic feedback—knowledge he can use to turn you on in the future.

The erotic feedback loop is an important part of talking sexy. You're not just taking turns speaking—you're creating an energy spiral. The more excitement you show, the more he'll want to excite you. You say something that turns him on, he responds with something that turns you on, and suddenly you're booked on an interplanetary flight.

Using sounds and words to indicate pleasure engages your partner in an erotic loop of sexual communication. Here's what happens when you don't engage:

Your partner kisses a hot spot for you—behind your ears.

You don't say a word or utter a sound, even though you like it.

He moves away from your hot spot and kisses a cold spot.

Here's what happens when you do engage:

Your partner kisses a hot spot—behind your ears.

You sigh and say, "Look at the goose bumps you're giving me."

He says, "Wow, I love what this does to you" and pays more attention to the spot.

You try to wriggle free and say, "Stop, I can't take much more of that."

Your partner moans, says, "Really...." and intensifies the feeling with gentle wet kisses.

You try to wiggle away, but he won't let you. And just as you surrender to the feeling, he blows softly in your ear and heats it with the warmth of his tongue. You say, "You're making me wet."

And it's a race to see who can tear off their clothes first…

This is how talking sexy ignites the erotic loop. You make a sound or say something. Your partner responds. His acknowledgement of your arousal arouses you. Your excitement excites him and soon you're both sucked up into a vortex of pleasure.

Verb Me! Verb Me Now!

Using coded words and couched language in place of graphic talk is fine, but it's a little like pedaling a bicycle to the party when you've got the keys to the Kawasaki. They'll both get you there, but only one will rock your world. Lusty carnal desires should be expressed with language equal to its intensity. *Vrrooooom!*

"Dirty" words are a funny thing. What offends you in day-to-day conversation may please you in the heat of passion. You'd be offended if you bumped into a stranger who called you a cunt, but you might be aroused if your partner said he *wanted your cunt* in the middle of a steamy session.

So how should you start? I'm not going to put words in your mouth—that would be unsanitary. You have no idea where my words have been. But more importantly, it doesn't matter what you say but the authenticity with which you say it. What's your truth? All you've got to do is state it. The objective isn't creativity, it's conductivity. How much heat can you conduct? There is no such thing as a must-use line (well, there is *one*, but that's later in the chapter).

If graphic sex talk still makes you uncomfortable, cloak the harsher, more startling phrases into warm, sensual questions or statements. For instance, instead of saying, "I want you to fuck me," you could say things like:

I want to feel you moving inside me.

Can you feel how wet and warm you've gotten me?

How to Overcome Self-Censorship

There's really only one thing that's stopping you from talking graphically in bed—you haven't given yourself permission to do it. Think of talking sexy as slipping into a new persona—the way you'd slip into a dress. Every woman knows how ditching warm-up pants for a sexy cocktail dress with (hopefully) a pair of Christian Louboutins can completely change your perspective. Talking dirty is like that. You're trying on a new outfit. And just as wearing a corporate suit doesn't make you a stuffed shirt, talking dirty doesn't make you a tramp. Talking sexy can be a reflection of who you are or who you never let out. Give yourself permission for a wardrobe change.

The Hottest Thing You Can Ever Say to a Guy

I lied. I said I wouldn't give you specific lines to use in bed. Well, there's one. Every survey that asks men what they like to hear women say in bed puts this phrase at the top of the charts:

I'm coming.

Part of the appeal is obvious: men get pleasure out of seeing your pleasure. Your partner wants to feel like a man, and nothing bears witness to his masculinity more than bringing you to orgasm. Okay, maybe he didn't bring you to orgasm, but he was in the room when it happened, and to the male ego it's the same thing.

Your orgasm is proof of his sexual powers. Saying "I'm coming" is a bit like playing "The Star Spangled Banner" before he receives the Olympic gold medal—it amps up the pivotal moment of victory. For attentive lovers who know that women should finish first, your announcement also signals permission that he can now come whenever he wants.

How to Say It in a Sexy Voice

Earlier I said it's not what you say but *that* you say. I'd like to amend that—it's also how you say it. The quality of your voice is as important as the content of your words. With the right voice we can get turned on by people reciting the alphabet. But what exactly are the qualities of a sexy voice, and how can you bring it forth and put your own personal stamp on it?

Most of us associate a sexy voice with deep, rich, throaty, husky sounds. There's a reason for that—it's what your voice sounds like after an orgasm. Experts call it the "postcoital voice" because the effects of an orgasm—the release of muscle tension, the change in hormones—move your breathing away from your chest and onto your diaphragm.

So, how can you re-create that "postcoital voice" in the bedroom? By practicing diaphragmatic breathing. You'll not only feel more calm and relaxed, but you'll also cultivate the rich, deep, husky sounds we associate with a sexy voice.

If you're like most people, you're a "high-chest" breather (your shoulders rise when you breathe). This can raise the larynx, set your whole vocal mechanism out of whack, and cause you to sound tense, rushed, and—frankly—a little irritating. By practicing diaphragmatic breathing (belly breathing), you can subtly and sometimes dramatically change your speaking voice.

So where's your diaphragm? Lie on your back (preferably on the floor). Notice how you're breathing. It's most likely from the chest. Place a small book on your stomach. Breathe in a way that moves the book up and down. That's diaphragmatic breathing. Remember this feeling, the breathing pattern, and activate it when you talk.

Another way to identify diaphragmatic breathing is to put your hand on your belly when you first wake up. It's natural to breathe with your belly. It's only when we wake and get all anxious that we shift the breathing to our chests.

Practice your postcoital voice by speaking as you expel breath with your belly. It will naturally lower the volume and the register of your voice. Here's a cool way to jump-start the process: Say the "h" in "he" without pronouncing the "e." Say something else within a second of starting the h sound and you'll be amazed at how it lowers the pitch of your voice.

Free Yourself from the Surly Bonds of Silence

Silence is a form of withdrawal that frees you to focus on perceived flaws. Talking is a form of participation that reduces the opportunity to self-focus. Talking sexy is all about participation and "energy management"—the ability to create, monitor, and master sexual energy. It can make you feel like the world is speeding up or ending more slowly. It heightens anticipation, magnifies sensations, and intensifies orgasms. It can also give your anxious thoughts a serious case of amnesia. By provocatively communicating your desires and expressing your love, you silence self-judgment and give voice to the depth, richness, and variety of your erotic feelings.

Talking sexy also improves your competency in bed. Men love to hear women talk dirty, and because they do, it's an important part of being a good sex partner—a critical goal for you because competency creates confidence, which kills judgment.

Think of talking in bed as caressing your lover with words. Entice, excite, enchant. Don't be captive to silence. Free your tongue, the zest will follow.

11

SEXUALLY FANTASIZING YOUR WAY OUT OF APPEARANCE ANXIETY

"Sometimes the only way I can get through sex is to fantasize I'm a beautiful woman with a perfect body. Sometimes I get so lost in the fantasy that my self-consciousness just disappears. And for extended moments in time, I actually make love to my partner without wondering if my hips are too big or whether he sees the pooch in my belly."

—Sharon, 41, Phoenix, Arizona

Fantasies remove you from reality. They lift your attention off the tarmac, leaving your anxieties at the gate with their noses pressed against the window. But scientists have only recently discovered that they lift something else, too: libidos.

Let me explain how they figured this out. For years, researchers have known that sexual thoughts increase arousal by elevating testosterone, a crucial hormone for female sexual functioning. For example, testosterone levels increase the day before women in long-distance relationships see their partners again.

There's a difference between anticipating sex with someone you're already intimate with (sexual thoughts) and daydreaming about making love with someone who may not even exist (fantasies). Sexual thoughts are based on experience, memory, and real-life triggers like wearing your partner's shirt to bed when he's gone. Fantasies are not. They are mostly made up of whole cloth.

Researchers wanted to know if fantasies had the same libido-raising properties of sexual thoughts, so they designed an experiment in which women were asked to imagine a positive sexual encounter with an attractive person. They intentionally did not specify the person nor the sexual activity to allow test subjects to self-define who or what turned them on. In other words, the women were asked to fantasize. The results were dramatic. As academics at the University of Michigan at Ann Arbor noted in their study in *Hormones and Behavior:*

> Women can influence their testosterone levels by simply thinking sexual thoughts...Our findings suggest that imagining a sexual encounter produces a similar testosterone response to actually engaging in sexual behavior.

Given these findings, it behooves you to cultivate your imagination—to find the hidden, unacknowledged, or undiscovered revelries that can make you sit up, stand tall...and swoon.

Imagination to the Rescue!

What exactly is a fantasy? It's your erotic imagination applied to people, places, and activities. Fantasies can make you feel empowered, playful, and excited. They let you experience things you might never allow yourself in real life. Where else but in your fantasies can you invite a parade of strangers into your bedroom without breaking your wedding vows? Where else can you sleep with your favorite movie star without your boyfriend knowing it? Where else can you have those two new guys at the gym making love to you without those two guys knowing about it? Many women don't realize how much fun has disappeared from their love lives until they activate their imagination.

The great thing about fantasies is that you can't get them wrong. They can be as elaborate as a romance novel or as spare as a single image, a scene, a recollection of a look or a touch that's especially meaningful to you.

How to Find Out What Your Fantasies Are

"But wait!" you might think, "I don't have any fantasies and I don't know how to get them." Just because you're not fully conscious of sexual fantasies doesn't mean you don't have them. You just haven't been able to access them. Most people start off by asking the wrong question. It's not "What's my fantasy?" It's *What turns me on?*"

Use physicality as the entry point to your imagination, then keep asking yourself the next logical questions. For example…

What turns me on?

Example: Being seduced slowly with delicate kisses and powerful hands.

Who turns me on?

Example: a powerful, intellectual man respected for his acumen and the way other men defer to him. If you draw a blank, ask yourself how you want to feel or how you want people to react to you in real life. Do you want to be adored or hated? Mistreated or worshipped? Then ask what type of person epitomizes that feeling to you.

What's the location?

Where do you want to do the things you say turn you on? In the desert, on the beach, down the stairs? On top of a car? And, ahem, exactly what would you do with the hood ornament?

Let me walk you through the type of questions you'd ask if your fantasy took place in a library.

What are the details?

What does it look like? What section do you want to do it

in? Reference? Special Collections? And hey, what about props or clothing? What is your dream man wearing? Something? Nothing? Prada? What do you smell? Musty books? His aftershave?

Who else is involved?

The librarian? Clark Kent? The New York Jets defensive lineup? Why are they there, and what do they want to do to you?

What do you want to experience?

Dominance, submission, something in between? Do you want to be opened up and searched like a reference book or smacked around by the Dewey decimal system? How do you want to be touched? Roughly? Softly? Do you want to be undressed or do the undressing? Be detailed. The more questions you ask, the deeper you can go in a fantasy, until you start discovering things you didn't even know you wanted.

The Most Common Sexual Fantasies for Women

There are a million different types of fantasies, but like sexual positions, there are only a few basic ones. The rest are variations guided by your own imagination. Below are the sexual themes that women gravitate toward.

- Being "taken" or dominated
- Being forced to have sex against your will
- Making love to an ex
- Having sex with somebody you know but never dated
- Incorporating romance into a sexual scene
- Dominating or having complete control over your partner
- Being the aggressor
- Sex with a male prostitute
- Being a prostitute
- Pretending to be another person—a celebrity, a model, a fictional character

- Having sex in a public place
- Doing it with more than one partner at a time (threesome, orgies, mate swapping)
- Running the risk of getting caught
- Having sex out in nature
- Having sex with a virgin
- Being a virgin
- Remembering past lovemaking
- Pretending you're a man
- Having sex with another woman
- Focusing on clothing, food, or nonsexual body parts
- Engaging in sexual positions or acts that you don't normally do
- Cross-dressing
- Having sex with a deity or spiritual leader
- Having sex with a forbidden or inappropriate figure

Fantasies for Body-Conscious Women

It's common for body-conscious women to fantasize themselves as the cover model of a *Sports Illustrated* swimsuit edition or an angel in a Victoria's Secret catalog. There's nothing wrong with fantasizing about having the kind of body you always wanted; just make sure you play the part correctly. Don't just pretend you have a sex kitten's face and body—pretend you have her mind-set. What would she do in bed? What would she say to your partner? How would she act? Make the fantasy complete.

Once, during a hot yoga class, I had a hard time standing at attention between poses. The room was warmed to 110 degrees. The teacher noticed my droopy posture and told me to throw back my shoulders, suck my stomach in, and stand straighter. "Act how you want to feel!" she commanded. In just a few seconds, I felt stronger, more capable, and ready for the next round. If you're going to fantasize about being Miss Thing, then take my yoga instructor's advice and *act how you want to feel.*

By the way, you don't have to tell your partner you're fantasizing. It's fine to keep it to yourself. In fact, one of the great appeals of a fantasy is that you don't have to share it if you don't want. The secretiveness itself is what makes it special.

Cheating on Your Partner with Your Partner

Fantasizing that you're with another man is an extraordinarily common fantasy, which unfortunately can bring up a bit of worry and guilt. Is it unfair or unethical to fantasize about another man while you're making love to your partner? Shouldn't he be enough to turn you on? Are you violating his trust?

No. It doesn't matter how you stoke your hunger as long as you eat at home. Anything you can do to increase sexual satisfaction and response within the confines of your relationship is a good thing. It's like asking if vibrators are an indictment on your sex life. Are you cheating on your partner if you use a rabbit? Are you cheating on him because you need the type of stimulation a hand can't provide? It's the same with fantasies. Are you cheating on him because you need mental stimulation he can't provide?

Some women won't let themselves indulge in fantasies about other men because they're afraid they'll get "addicted" to it. That's like avoiding sex toys because they might replace your partner. Do not ever feel guilty about using things or ideas that draw you closer. Fantasies, like sex toys, are not replacements; they're add-ons.

It's All in Your Head

Fantasies have many roles. One of them is to reconcile inner conflicts. Forced sex is a common and often disturbing fantasy for a lot of women. Many question what it says about them, giving rise to fear and self-judgment. Many theorists believe that rape is a common fantasy for women not because they actually want to be raped but because it solves the double-standard imposed on them: Look sexual but don't be sexual. If sex is forced on you, then you can't be judged or feel guilty about having it.

Another theory is that being forcibly taken proves your sexual desirability. After all, who's going to force themselves on an unattractive woman? The fantasy isn't so much about rape as it is experiencing the feeling that you're so desirable that men can't control themselves when they're around you.

Of course, sometimes a cigar is just a cigar. Sometimes the fantasy really is all about force, but that doesn't necessarily mean you want to experience it in real life. So, relax. Buy some popcorn and enjoy the movie.

How to Poach a Fantasy When You Can't Come Up with Your Own

"When I was young I used to pray for a bike," a girlfriend once told me. "Then I realized that God doesn't work that way, so I stole a bike and prayed for forgiveness." For some women, fantasies are like my girlfriend's bike—you're better off stealing than praying for them. If you truly can't come up with your own fantasies, there are plenty of places to steal a little creativity and call them your own.

Hooray for Hollywood

Over the years, Tinsel Town has produced some of the most extraordinary sex scenes imaginable. This is better news than you think—studies have found that women's testosterone levels increase after watching a romantic film and imagining themselves as the actress being wooed by the attractive man. I've assembled my list of the top ten hottest sex scenes in modern movie history below. Imagine yourself as one of the characters, and you'll be swept away by the sheer force of the sexual currents. Do you want some butter with that popcorn?

1. *The Big Easy* (1987)
2. *End of the Affair* (1999)
3. *Mulholland Drive* (2001)
4. *9 1/2 Weeks* (1986)
5. *Coming Home* (1978)

6. *Henry and June* (1990)
7. *Body Heat* (1982)
8. *Unfaithful* (2002)
9. *Y Tu Mamá También* (2001)
10. *Don't Look Now* (1973)

If you want to get more juice out of a movie than simply inhabiting the characters, just ask yourself a few questions. What would make this scene even hotter for me? What would I change? What would I add or subtract? Where else would I let Mickey Rourke squirt the honey?

To porn or not to porn?

Women have a prickly relationship with porn. On the one hand, studies show that watching erotic films increases genital blood flow. On the other hand, they *failed* to show that they elevate testosterone.

At the beginning of this chapter, I mentioned studies proving that fantasies, unlike erotic films, increase the production of testosterone. Why would engaging a fantasy elevate more testosterone than watching porn? Studies suggest that *psychological* sexual arousal is necessary for testosterone levels to rise, explaining why women have such an ambivalent reaction to porn. On the one hand, it is physiologically arousing—as evidenced by genital blood flow. But unless the film has specific elements that speak to women, it is rarely psychologically arousing—as evidenced by the lack of elevated testosterone.

Pick your porn

Once, a rather conservative, religious friend of mine checked into a hotel and asked if the porn channel in his room was disabled. The clerk said, "No, it's regular porn, you sick bastard." You might be like my friend and find all porn offensive, or you could be like the clerk and only find certain types that are out of bounds.

Either way, the research argues for using erotic films that are psychologically arousing *to you*. Be careful with the typical male *bomp-chicka-wow-wow* flicks. You may get physically excited because you're witnessing skin-to-skin contact, but are you psychologically aroused? It's unlikely that made-for-men porn will do the trick because it lacks so much of what typically arouses women: intimacy, attractive men, appealing sex acts, sexual tension, interesting dialogue, foreplay, kissing, the list goes on. And don't even start with the women. From their nails to their hair to their makeup, the women in these videos seem as fake as a Thai Rolex.

Women-centered porn, on the other hand, has everything that turns women on: credible actors, emotion-infused sex, attentive men, authentic stories, genuine chemistry, interesting locations, and yes, real women's orgasms. They also feature something you rarely see in men's porn: women with a wide variety of shapes and sizes.

To find the most current women-centered porn, head to www.goodforher.com, which produces an annual "feminist porn awards show." And for a comprehensive list of women-centered erotica, visit www.pornmoviesforwomen.com.

In the meantime, here's my list of the must-see classics:

1. *Afrodite Superstar*
2. *Trial Run*
3. *Pirates*
4. *Uniform Behavior*
5. *Insatiable*
6. *Fashion Underground*
7. *Edge Play*
8. *Chemistry*
9. *Night Trips*
10. *Paid Companions*

The pen is mightier than the sword

Sometimes you're just a page away from having the fantasy of your life. Pick up a book like Nancy Friday's *My Secret Garden*, and you'll find a treasure trove of fantasies and sexual dreams that hundreds of women shared with the author.

For even more flights of fancy, read erotica specifically written by and for women. Many wonder about the distinction between erotica and porn. Porn is a straight, in-your-face (and other orifices) accounting of sex for sex's sake. Erotica is more of an artist's rendering of sex. While it includes sexually explicit descriptions, it infuses it with love, romance, and three-dimensional characters. Erotica is porn with artistic merit.

Try reading any of the books below and you'll fire up your imagination faster than a sex toy with a kick-start.

Erotic literature that got the authors prosecuted for obscenity

Lady Chatterley's Lover, D. H. Lawrence
Madame Bovary, Gustave Flaubert
The God of Small Things, Arundhati Roy
The Flowers of Evil, Charles Baudelaire
Tropic of Cancer, Henry Miller
Fanny Hill, or Memoirs of a Woman of Pleasure, John Cleland

Erotic literature that didn't get authors in trouble

Fifty Shades of Grey, E. L. James
Boys and Girls Together, William Goldman
Candy, Maxwell Kenton
The Carpetbaggers, Harold Robbins
Couples, John Updike
Diary of Anais Nin, Anais Nin
Doctor Zhivago, Boris Pasternak
The Four-Gated City, Doris Lessing
The French Lieutenant's Woman, John Fowles
The Group, Mary McCarthy
The Happy Hooker, Xaviera Hollander
Love Poems, Anne Sexton
The Pearl, Anonymous
The Perfumed Garden of the Sheikh Nefzaoui, Anonymous

Romeo and Juliet, William Shakespeare
The Sensuous Couple, Robert Chartham
The Sensuous Woman, "J"
The Story of O, Pauline Reage
Tender Is the Night, F. Scott Fitzgerald
Valley of the Dolls, Jacqueline Susann
The Virgin and the Gypsy, D. H. Lawrence

Collections of real people's fantasies

My Secret Garden, Nancy Friday
Forbidden Flowers: More Women's Sexual Fantasies, Nancy Friday
Men In Love (Men's Sexual Fantasies), Nancy Friday

Erotica

Best Women's Erotica 2011, Violet Blue, editor
Orgasmic: Erotica for Women, Rachel Kramer Bussel, editor
Sweet Confessions: Erotic Fantasies for Couples, Violet Blue, editor
Playing With Fire: Taboo Erotica, Alison Tyler, editor
Lust: Erotic Fantasies for Women, Violet Blue, editor
Passion: Erotic Romance for Women, Rachel Kramer Bussel, editor
Just Watch Me: Erotica for Women, Violet Blue, editor
Enchanted: Erotic Bedtime Stories for Women, Nancy Madore, editor
Literotica 2: The Very Best of Literotica.com
Fast Girls: Erotica for Women, Rachel Kramer Bussel, editor
Bedtime Erotica, Lexy Harper, editor
Frenzy: 60 Stories of Sudden Sex, Alison Tyler, editor
X: The Erotic Treasury, Susie Bright, editor
Please, Sir: Erotic Stories of Female Submission, Rachel Kramer Bussel, editor

A picture is worth a thousand *ooohs*

Erotic photography books have the power to transport you into a different plane of existence. The very best of these books are single-photo tales of lust, voyeurism, and seduction that mix sweeping cinematic images with majestic backdrops. Or not. Some are just plain hot. Tantalize yourself with the subtle and not-so-subtle allusions to sex in the photographic compilations of the books listed below.

Women, celebrities, and couples

The New Erotic Photography, Dian Hanson, Eric Kroll
Erotique: Masterpieces of Erotic Art, Michelle Olley
Monica Bellucci, Monica Bellucci, Giuseppe Tornatore
Ellen von Unwerth: Fraulein, Ingrid Sischy and Ellen von Unwerth
Ingrid Sischy, Ellen von Unwerth
The Morning After, David Drebin
Herb Ritts: L.A. Style, Paul Martineau and James Crump

Men

Naked, Dylan Rosser
Heroics, Paul Freeman
Turnon: Sports: The Best in Erotic Sports Photography, Bruno Gmunder Verlag
Players, Rick Day
Wet Men, Francois Rousseau
Dieux du Stade: Gods of the Stadium, Tony Duran
Supersized, Giovanni
Oversized, Stephan Niederwieser, Simeon Morales
Luminosity, Mark Henderson
Black and Beautiful, Peter Arnold

Turning Solo Fantasies into Partner-Friendly Activities

So far, we've discovered dozens of ways to fire up the imagination, but we've limited them to your own mind. It's time to share them with your partner. This can be a little awkward for body-conscious women who've been avoiding sex. The easiest way to start a conversation is to buy a book like *Lust: Erotic Fantasies for Women*, press it into your partner's hand, and say, "Why don't you take a look at the passages I've underlined and let's talk about it at dinner."

If you don't have that sort of personality, you can always tuck the book into your partner's briefcase or surreptitiously leave it in his car with a note. The advantage of "placing" the book for discovery is that you don't have to be in charge of bringing up the subject and bringing it to a head, as it were.

Still, to avoid any awkwardness about what should be done next, you should know that the best way to share a fantasy with your partner is to...

Read to each other

Nothing will jump-start your sexual feelings more than hearing the timbre in your partner's voice when he reads some of your favorite passages in the erotica books listed below. It can bring sex alive in ways you've never experienced. Conversely, reading to him may do it even more for you, especially if you're not used to "talking dirty." Take turns reading and make sure you're touching each other when you do—you'll feel more sexually and emotionally connected.

As you read the books, be aware of favorite passages—yours and his. They are the single-engine planes that help you take off into parts unknown. It doesn't take long to uncover "trigger themes"— storylines, actions, characters, and activities that stir up ravenous sexual hunger.

Ask him to kiss and caress you while you read your favorite passage out loud. Be explicit as to how and where you want to be touched. This is about pleasure—your pleasure—and the only way to get it is to ask for it.

Be sure to return the favor—caress him sensually as he reads his favorite passages, and if he doesn't tell you how or where he wants to be touched, ask him. You can't be competent without communication. And remember, we're always seeking competency because it's the only thing that earns you confidence, which in turn raises your libido and the satisfaction you will get from sex.

For a more sophisticated—and fun—variation of reading to each other, put down the book in mid-story and continue the tale as if you were both the central characters in it. Make it up as you go along and take note of when your partner gets particularly worked up. This is part of your competency training—understanding what turns him on.

The erotic telephone game

As a child, you probably remember playing "the telephone game," where you whisper a short sentence into someone's ear and they would in turn whisper it to the person sitting next to them. By the time the message got through a dozen kids the story got so twisted around everybody laughed at the last telling. Well, in this game, there are only two players and nobody laughs at the end because they're too busy getting busy.

Here's how it works: Tell your partner a story. Start with "Once upon a time" then follow it up with a sentence or two from one of your fantasies (or erotica stories). Then your partner adds the next sentence with something that turns him on. Back and forth you go, the story veering from your fantasy to his until it blends into one superhighway going in the same direction—south of the border.

Creating three-dimensional fantasies

Once you get comfortable with solo and spoken-word fantasies, the next step is to act them out, to make them as three-dimensional as possible. The easiest way to start is with role-play.

Role-playing means inhabiting the characters and situations in your imagination. It puts the "lay" in play. It eases you into spontaneity and playfulness with a great expansion of your sexual horizons. And it is especially useful for the body conscious because so much of the emphasis is on leaving who you are to become someone you're not. Finally, taking on a new character might just give you the confidence to try things you may have always shied away from. Thinking and acting differently usually produces different results in bed.

The first step in role-play isn't to pick the role you want to play; it's to pick the experience you want to have. Do you want to be cherished and adored or disrespected and debilitated? Does innocence part your waters or does evil do the job? Do you want to feel aggression or serve it up? Do you want to hurt or do the hurting? Do you want power coursing through your veins? Nearly any character you assume will give you the chops to experience all that and more. The next step is to figure out what characters or scenes fascinate you. It can be anyone—real or imagined, from the past, present, or future. They can share your values or flout them at every turn. They can make you feel good or bad, kind or mean, intelligent or stupid. If you can't think of anyone (or anything), try somebody (or something) from the list below.

- Celebrities
- Doctor
- Exotic dancer
- Extraterrestrials
- Fictional characters from your favorite books
- Film director
- Gangster
- Gods and goddesses
- Historical figures
- Hooker
- Hypnotist
- Magician
- Nurse
- Patient
- Pirate
- Police officer
- Politicians
- Porn star
- Sex therapist
- Student
- Teacher
- Virgin

Okay, now you know what you want to experience and what characters you want to experience them through. Next, ask yourself what role your partner needs to play in order for you to experience what you want to feel. In fact, every question you ask yourself should be some version of, *What will make this more real for me?* Costumes and props will help you get into character while music sets the scene and the mood. If you're doing a master-slave scene, for example, I don't think preadolescent boy-band music is going to add much. The more detail you can put in a scene, the more real it will be. The question we dwelled on in the cultivating sensuality chapter applies here: *What can I do to enhance the sensations I'm feeling?* In this realm, there is no right or wrong. Only helpful or unhelpful.

Keep the fantasy going forward by taking control of it. For example, if you want your partner to strip, somebody's got to decide how. I say if it's your fantasy, you be the boss. Now, what if your partner doesn't share your fantasy? You get around it by taking turns. You can be the supporting actress in his fantasy and the star in yours.

Cover your eyes so your mind can see

Fantasies don't require exotic locales, uniforms, or even role-play. Sometimes all they require is covering your eyes so your mind can see. Blindfolds, for example, are an uncanny way of turning the familiar into the mysterious. Try blindfolding each other in bed. By subtracting one sense, blindfolds require the other four to work harder. Without vision, two hands can feel like four or six. The intriguing part is that you don't know where the next touch or probe is going to come from. Sensations are heightened and here's the best part: Everybody looks like a million bucks!

So here's how it works: You and your partner blindfold yourselves and sit naked on the opposite corners of the bed. On a whispery count of three, slowly advance toward each other. Touch, explore, discover. What do you do? Where do you go? You don't know. That's the point. If neither of you can see each other's facial expressions during the action, it'll leave you with a tingling curiosity: "What's he thinking?" "What's she feeling?" Think of it as a blank canvas for the imagination. By depriving yourselves of sight, you create anticipation and heighten the senses. When that happens, every position is a new position—unless darkness works its mischief and you knock him off the bed or he calls you by the wrong name.

How to Handle Sharing or Hearing Disturbing Fantasies

Disclosing a fantasy, no matter how trivial or dark, is a bit like a trapeze act—you jump off the ledge in complete vulnerability and hope to hell your partner's hands are there waiting for you when you come out of the flip.

Having a session of Fantasy Confessions requires an emotional safety net. Agree to listen without judgment, shame, or ridicule, and save the potentially troublesome fantasies for another session. It's best to build a reservoir of trust and safety before disclosing something that might be disturbing.

It's one thing if your sexual fantasy is to make it with a goat herder; another with his herd. The first might evoke a chuckle, the second a pillow and sheets for the couch. How do you know where to draw the line on sharing? Easy. No mention of the illegal or the immoral. And, please, no goats.

Still, sometimes things slip out, and once they're out you have to deal with them. If they do, remember that the vast majority of "dangerous" fantasies are just that—fantasies that don't want to see the light of day in the real world. Most people who harbor illegal, immoral, or otherwise shocking fantasies have them because they're intrigued with the forbidden. Often, it's the unconscious mind harboring them as metaphors to get at what the conscious mind cannot access directly. And even when it's not a metaphor or a vehicle to work something out, people who have darker imaginings want the liberation of experiencing it in their minds so they don't have to deal with the real-life consequences. They are arousing precisely because they are forbidden and because people would never allow themselves to actually do them.

If you hear a disturbing fantasy, you could do worse than remembering that giving or experiencing a lover's acceptance is one of the most healing aspects of being in a relationship. Simply reaffirming love in the face of distressing news helps integrate the disowned parts of ourselves and deepen our emotional bonds.

Imagine This

Scientists have proven that fantasies—*simply having sexual thoughts*—can elevate testosterone levels in women. This is a double blessing for body-conscious women because fantasies can simultaneously raise your libido and pry the fingers of anxiety off your mind.

Depending on your ability to suspend disbelief, the human mind can transform you or your partner into someone else. This is your opportunity to step outside of yourself, to be someone you always wanted to be, to feel things you always wanted to experience, and get yourself in situations that are exciting and fun.

For example, look at your bedroom. It's a place you sleep, right? Bed, lamps, end tables, maybe a chair. But your imagination can turn a simple bedroom into a lair. What if every Sunday night between nine and midnight the bedroom became a bubble? And on the appointed time and date you step through the bubble into a fantasyland where you get to explore inhabiting different people with your partner? Or maybe you put a little effort into transforming a room. Maybe you cover the living room furniture with white sheets, move everything to the side, lay a futon in the middle of it, and circle it with candles to create the look of a sexual altar?

Fantasies are the easiest and most powerful way to gain a deeper understanding of who you are and what you need. And the great thing is, there are no rules or boundaries. Fantasies share something with infinity: There are no limits, only plateaus.

PLAYING WITH POWER

"I wish I could just press the stop button and enjoy sex the way I used to before I gained all this weight. Now, all I do is hide, avoid, or make excuses. I feel disconnected from my body and my husband."

—Jessica, 37, Seattle, Washington

As you saw earlier, fantasy operates a busy transportation hub in your mind, capable of projecting you to its different territories without so much as an overnight bag. Well, there's a second, related hub that can take you deeper underground where the treasure is buried—playing with power.

You play with power all the time, you just never labeled it that way. If you like to be pinned under your guy, you've experienced the thrill of submitting to power. If you like holding him down, you've experienced the thrill of wielding it. It's not possible to have sex without some kind of power exchange. At one moment or another you are wielding or yielding.

If you're doing missionary, you are surrendering yourself to him. If you're on top guiding the speed and depth of his thrusts, you're controlling him. If you dig your nails into his back, you've inflicted pain. If he does it, you've had pain inflicted on you. If you've liked a massage that almost hurts, you've experienced a pleasurable aspect of pain. If you've given one, you've experienced the satisfaction of administering it.

Just because you're not conscious of how you relate to and enjoy power doesn't mean you're not experiencing it. In fact, the only difference between power playing and *structured* power playing is awareness and intent. For example, you might not have intended to have your partner spank you when you got into that playful wrestling match. And you might not have been aware that the pleasant sensations you experienced came from yielding to his power.

With *structured* power playing, on the other hand, you come at it with awareness and intent. You become aware that you like to be lightly spanked (or do the spanking), get your partner's agreement to participate, and create the environment for a satisfying experience. It is an organized, systematic attempt at creating the power sensations you're drawn to.

You Have No Choice but to Submit

The key to structured power playing is the exchange of power or sensation (spanking, being tied up). You can be submissive (choosing to allow the other person to have control over you in some way) or dominant (choosing to honor the request of the submissive). Notice the words "choose" and "allow." They are critical to consensual, structured power playing.

Power playing is a terrific way of leaving your appearance anxieties on hold. Submitting to power, for example, often elicits an exhilarating, liberating feeling. By giving up responsibility for what's going on, by bending your will to the authority of another, by taking on the role of the compliant and the helpless, you can experience a form of therapeutic escape, not just from your appearance obsession, but from everything else—stress, guilt, shame, fear, and anger.

Being in the presence of a controlling figure makes some people feel the kind of safety and protection they felt as a child. Others like the feeling of surrendering themselves, of disappearing into the unavoidable nothingness that comes from relinquishing all power. Still others like earning the approval of a dominant figure or turning their partner into somebody more commanding and powerful. Anastasia Steele, the main character in *Fifty Shades of Grey*, is a great example of a woman who came to embrace her inner submissive. Her love affair was so defined by structured power playing that she signed a dominance/submission contract with her lover, Christian Grey.

Command and Control

Taking the dominant position, on the other hand, provides the thrill that comes from placing yourself above someone else. You can enjoy the authority of telling someone what to do, watching them obey, inflicting "punishment" if they don't, and getting a vicarious thrill from seeing their "suffering."

Structured power playing is an exploration of your sexuality and personal boundaries. It's a way to play up excitement and intensity of the sexual experience. It transports you out of judgmental thoughts into territory that widens and deepens your understanding of who you are. It's hard to dredge up judgments about your appearance when you're in the middle of a passionate, personal sexual odyssey. Playing with power is the ultimate form of *participation*—the key to limiting your self-focus.

Ready, Set, Play!

It's easy to start power playing in a more intentional way—build on what you already like. For example, if you like it when your partner gently pins your hands over your head, then the next time it happens, tell him how much you like it and suggest that you go a bit further. Have some silk scarves by the nightstand and suggest that he tie you up gently.

Of course, this only works if you have a willing partner. If yours has a little too much starch in his collar, it's best to have a talk first so you don't scare the hair right off his head.

But let's get back to you being tied up with those scarves. What do you feel? How does he react? Do you like it? Which part? Why? Do you want to go further or dial it back? What would make it more arousing? What do you want him to say? What do you want him to do?

If things go well, you may discover that you want to go further next time, either with manacles or rope. If they didn't go well, no biggie, you just found out it's not for you. Or maybe it is, but it's you who should be tying the knots! Be sure to spark a conversation about other fantasies. This is your opportunity to shop the sample sale of your innermost desires. Of course, it can be a little challenging to understand what it is exactly that appeals to you. That's why you should...

Take Your Erotic Temperature

Sit down with your partner and circle the appropriate temperature for each power play suggestion below. Make sure you both do this at opposite ends of the house—don't try to influence each other. At least not yet. And don't worry about overlapping or contradictory preferences or trying to identify yourself either as a submissive or dominant. You can, for example, prefer to be submissive during a kiss and dominant during intercourse. Submission and domination can be traded and played with like cards. We're looking for opportunities, not labels.

Submissive Power Preferences

I prefer to receive rather than give.

Cold   Cool   Lukewarm   Warm   HOT

I like being on the bottom during romantic activity like kissing or intercourse.

Cold   Cool   Lukewarm   Warm   HOT

I like being told what to do in bed.

Cold   Cool   Lukewarm   Warm   HOT

I like surrendering control.

Cold   Cool   Lukewarm   Warm   HOT

I like feeling protected by my partner.

Cold   Cool   Lukewarm   Warm   HOT

I like it when my partner takes the lead and shows a bit of aggression.

Cold   Cool   Lukewarm   Warm   HOT

I like it when my partner is powerful and commanding in bed.

Cold   Cool   Lukewarm   Warm   HOT

I like obeying my partner's sexual instructions.

Cold   Cool   Lukewarm   Warm   HOT

I like intercourse a little bit on the rough side.

Cold   Cool   Lukewarm   Warm   HOT

I like it when my partner comes close to verbally insulting me in bed.

Cold   Cool   Lukewarm   Warm   HOT

I like feeling possessed by my partner.

Cold   Cool   Lukewarm   Warm   HOT

I like it when my partner partially or fully immobilizes me with his hands and feet.

Cold   Cool   Lukewarm   Warm   HOT

I like it when my partner pinches, squeezes, holds, or otherwise touches me in a forceful way.

Cold   Cool   Lukewarm   Warm   HOT

I like to be the recipient of "angry" sex.

Cold   Cool   Lukewarm   Warm   HOT

I like it when my partner comes close to hurting me during sex.

Cold   Cool   Lukewarm   Warm   HOT

I like it when my partner acts as if he's punishing me with sex.

Cold   Cool   Lukewarm   Warm   HOT

Dominant Power Preferences

I prefer to give rather than receive.

Cold   Cool   Lukewarm   Warm   HOT

I like being on top during romantic activity.

Cold   Cool   Lukewarm   Warm   HOT

I like telling my partner what to do in bed.

Cold   Cool   Lukewarm   Warm   HOT

I like exerting control.

Cold   Cool   Lukewarm   Warm   HOT

I like feeling like my partner's protector.

Cold   Cool   Lukewarm   Warm   HOT

I like taking the lead and showing a bit of aggression.

Cold   Cool   Lukewarm   Warm   HOT

I like being powerful and commanding in bed.

Cold   Cool   Lukewarm   Warm   HOT

I like seeing my partner obey my sexual instructions.

Cold   Cool   Lukewarm   Warm   HOT

I like sex a bit on the rough side.

Cold   Cool   Lukewarm   Warm   HOT

I like coming close to verbally insulting my partner in bed.

Cold   Cool   Lukewarm   Warm   HOT

I like the feeling of possessing my partner.

Cold   Cool   Lukewarm   Warm   HOT

I like to partially or fully immobilize my partner with my hands and feet.

Cold   Cool   Lukewarm   Warm   HOT

I like to pinch, squeeze, hold, or otherwise touch my partner in a forceful way.

Cold   Cool   Lukewarm   Warm   HOT

I like doling out "angry" sex.

Cold   Cool   Lukewarm   Warm   HOT

I like to come close to hurting my partner during sex.

Cold   Cool   Lukewarm   Warm   HOT

I like to "punish" my partner with sex.

Cold   Cool   Lukewarm   Warm   HOT

Free Your Mind, Your Crotch Will Follow

Done? Great! Now, take each other's lists and compare them. But before you do, brace yourself. You may be surprised at what your partner has circled. Sometimes the shyest guys have a secret wish to dominate and sometimes the most dominating personalities yearn to be taught a few lessons.

But enough about him. The point of this exercise is to get a clear picture of what turns *you* on so you can share it with your partner. Let this be the start of a conversation that allows you to have fun, push boundaries, and explore some areas of your own psychology.

The first step is identifying what you have in common and taking the next step forward. For example, if you circled HOT under "I like to partially or fully immobilize my partner with my hands and feet" and he matched you, then your next question to each other is, "How can we take this to the next level?"

The answer is anything from silk scarves to ropes to manacles or anything that pops into your head. Don't get stuck on the "right" answer—there is none. The only "right" answer is the one you feel comfortable with. Sit down together and create sexual scenarios that give you the power imbalance you crave. Once you decide to take it to the next level, your fantasies will take over and you'll begin to answer for yourself the question of how to go about it. If you're really stuck, try reading *Fifty Shades of Grey*, the Club Shadowlands series, or my personal favorite, *Screw the Roses, Send Me the Thorns*. For now, know that how, what, when, or where take a backseat to *why*. The important thing is discovering *why* you want to do this, not in how it gets accomplished. The why is because it turns you on. There's no better why in the world.

Learning the Ropes

Once you've both agreed on a specific power play to put some structure around, think about looking the part, setting the scene, and, ahem, learning the ropes. Always start slow, and if you're comfortable, ramp it up. Start safe, play sane, and build slowly. If it's all agreeable, then off you go to the next level. Always talk to your partner after you're done. Nothing new should ever be attempted without a debriefing. How'd you both feel? What turned you on or off? What would you want to explore later? Sometimes people respond in ways they didn't expect. You could look forward to trying something only to have it trigger negative feelings you hadn't anticipated. Don't judge it; accept it as a natural consequence of experimentation. Right now everything is flight data for the trip. Learn from it and set a new path. This brings up one of my guiding principles to good sex: Never try anything once. Try it three times. The first time you'll get it wrong, the second time it'll feel awkward, and the third time you'll truly know whether it's for you.

Lastly, don't feel that you have to try everything all at once. Go too fast too soon and you'll kick yourself right out the door. You've got plenty of time. This is an exploration, not a race.

Nobody finds buried treasure by rushing. You're exploring what turns you on, what turns your partner on, and what you can build together. You're better off ending a scene thinking you could have gone further than ending a scene thinking you went too far.

No matter what power playing preference you experiment with, it's important to concentrate on what really matters. It's not necessarily the scene you construct or even the physical sensations you feel. It's the experience of wielding or yielding to power.

Exploring a new dimension in your sex life means playing with that thing between your ears, not your legs. So as you experiment with different activities, embrace the power playing role you take on and understand what drives it. For example, if you assume the dominant role...

Concentrate on the pleasures of being in complete control

That means enjoying power and the status accrued to it. You create the scenario in any way you want. Why? *Because you said so*, that's why! You're the scriptwriter, director, and producer in charge of your submissive's fate. Taking charge takes some work, though. You have to have the dual ability to create your own fantasy while taking into account your partner's wishes. You have to be in command of the action but in tune with your partner. Otherwise, you won't sense when you've gone too far. Trust isn't free; it's earned by respecting limits.

Dominating your partner doesn't mean bending them to your will. It means bending them to *their* will—giving them what they've allowed you to give. Dishing out punishment to somebody who didn't ask for it is cruel. Dishing it out to somebody who did is fun. In that sense, the dominant is guided by the submissive. Pleasing your partner is omnidirectional in sexual power playing. The submissive takes pleasure from gratifying the needs of the dominant, and the dominant returns the favor.

Even in sensation-heavy scenarios like restraint or playful pain, the creamy center is always in the psychological arena. It doesn't matter if you're tying the knots in the right way; what matters is who you are as you're tying them and what feelings come up as you experience total control over somebody.

The same dynamic applies to any scene where you become the dominatrix. It doesn't matter what you boss him into. Being pushy isn't the point. Anybody can say, "Take your shirt off slowly... no, slower . . ." The delight isn't in the orders you give him but in watching him obey your every command. Don't be diverted by the idea that you're not bossing him around in the right way or spanking him in the right spot—those are skills you can get better at. Concentrate on the *interaction*, for it is there that you'll find the lickable, sensual intensity that is the promise of power playing.

The same applies if you take the submissive role. Then, it's important to...

Concentrate on the pleasures of surrendering

No matter what scene you construct out of your power playing preferences, your role as the submissive is to give up responsibility for what's going on, to step into the role created for you. You don't ever have to worry about your physical or emotional safety because your limits have been communicated and agreed to by the dominant. Because you decide what places can and cannot be explored, you can call a halt to everything at a second's notice. This knowledge gives you the ability to fully let go, to surrender to what happens next, without having any responsibility for it.

As noted before, the creamy center isn't necessarily in the details. If you're getting tied up, you may or may not like the feel of a scarf or a rope against your skin, but you'll love the physical sensation of being confined. It's a form of erotic helplessness. It's knowing that you have no choice but to submit, that your lover has free rein over your body. It might even give you permission to enjoy what you normally wouldn't allow yourself to enjoy. ("*What could I do? I had no choice. I was tied up.*")

Was It Good for You?

Context is everything. Getting a light spanking when you're aroused feels different than getting it when you're not. Even pleasant sensations are contextual. Getting your back scratched, for example, can feel yummy, neutral, or downright awful depending on the circumstances. It's great if you're comfortable, awful if you're sweating. It's a turn-on if the *Playgirl* centerfold does the scratching; a turn-off if it's Quasimodo. It's a relief if you have a mosquito bite; a terror if you have a sunburn.

Every form of stimulation is context-dependent, and pain is no exception. The right kind of pain with the right kind of buildup from the right kind of person during the right state of arousal can be the hottest thing you'll ever experience. It is well known that pain releases endorphins, a brain chemical that leads to euphoria. It's primarily responsible for the "runner's high" that comes with prolonged exercise. You can also see it at work when you eat chili peppers. The spicier the pepper, the more your body secretes endorphins. It doesn't mean you should run out and eat five-alarm chili peppers, but it does explain why some people are drawn to pain.

Endorphin release varies from person to person. Two people doing the same type of exercise or suffering from the same degree of pain will not necessarily produce the same levels of endorphins. That is a major reason why some people find pain (in the right context) highly arousing and others don't.

From a psychological point of view, pain forces out all other thoughts, feelings, and stresses. It gets your attention and makes you focus. This is clearly an advantage for the body conscious, but that's not to say it's specifically right for you. If you want to find out, there's a right way and a wrong way of going about it.

The wrong way is to take pain out of context. It will only be pleasant if you're near the throes of ecstasy. Do not get slapped, smacked, or spanked *unless you're aroused*. Otherwise, it will hurt like hell. Pain is contextual. Sexual arousal changes the perception of pain. Taking a bite out of a hot pepper is going to be a completely different experience than tasting the right amount of it in a plate of chili.

So how do you make sure you're tasting the chili and not biting the pepper? By making sure your partner knows to apply pain when you're *already* aroused, *after* he's created anticipation and is building toward a climax. That means making out, rolling around, and engaging in some heavy foreplay before a hand is raised or a tushy is bared. Start with mild sensations and build gradually to stronger sensations. It's the buildup that starts releasing the endorphins that change your perception of more intense pain. You don't get a runner's high on mile 2. It takes time. A spanking without buildup is going to hurt. A spanking after a slow buildup can make you slap happy.

If you're the dominant in a pain play scene like spanking (you wouldn't be the first girlie-girl to discover her inner dominatrix), ask for feedback. Pay attention to how he responds. This is as much an exploration for the giver as the receiver. Get to know what your partner likes so you can gauge what's too little and what's too much. If you find that neither one of you gets turned on, don't worry. You can always resort to the most conventional application of pain—calling tech support when the cable goes out.

Keeping Yourself Emotionally (and Physically) Safe

Set limits. Whoever chooses the submissive role needs to negotiate "hard" and "soft" limits. Hard limits are things you will absolutely not do under any circumstances. Soft limits are things you wouldn't do even in typical circumstances but would if the context and level of arousal changes. You set these limits for your own protection. You will save yourself a lot of grief by setting limits at a lower threshold, having a good experience, and raising them later rather than setting them high, having a bad experience, and then lowering them.

Set limits by asking questions. If your partner is the submissive and wants a bit of light pain, is it purely the physical sensation of being hit that he's looking for or is it to feel like he's being punished for some made-up transgression like violating the head-mistress's curfew? Does he want a couple of thwacks on the arm, or does he want to be smacked like a housefly? Negotiating this level of detail beforehand may feel a little awkward, but it'll save you some enormously unpleasant consequences.

"Consensual nonconsensuality" is an important principle in sexual power playing. You must voluntarily give up your right to say no *and* have the ability to immediately stop the action whenever you want. You do that by granting consent before the action begins and agreeing on a "safe word" that immediately stops the action, breaks the illusion, and returns you to reality.

What consent are you granting? Spell it out carefully. And what "safe word" immediately suspends the action? Communicate it clearly. A safe word is a mutually understood word that, when uttered, means *stop what you're doing right now*. It's like a movie director saying, "Cut!" Everybody instantly drops their role-playing.

Don't pick the word "no" or "stop" because part of the thrill may be to struggle against whatever is happening to you. Sort of like when guys are handed a broom and cleaning supplies so they can help with the housework. They'll shriek "No! No! No!" but, really, it just means they want more.

Safe words break the action without breaking the mood. They also allow the action to continue once the requisite strap is adjusted or the muscle cramp massaged away. Pick a safe word that's totally out of context, like "apple" or "book"—or if you really want to be stopped in your tracks, "Al Gore."

Safe words can be a simple on/off switch or a more multitiered set of signals such as "red" ("please stop right this instant"), "yellow" ("proceed with caution"), and "green" ("full steam ahead!").

Practice the golden rule

New activities should be accompanied by a pre-show role reversal. If your partner wants you to punish him with a ping-pong paddle, have him give you a couple of whacks to see exactly how he wants you to do it. It's easier to adjust the intensity if you know what it feels like.

Plan for the afterglow

Some activities can be a bit more intense than anticipated, leaving you, your partner, or both feeling a little out of sorts. Don't roll over and go to sleep right away. Plan to bring the mood down slowly and gently. Have a talk, a cuddle, a snack. Special takeoffs deserve special landings.

Don't die wondering

Sometimes people are afraid that if they experiment with structured power playing they'll walk through a door that will lock behind them. They're afraid they won't want to go back to "normal" sex, that they'll always hunger for something more. It's understandable to be apprehensive, but stopping yourself from experimenting is a little like saying you don't want to taste wine because you'll end up an alcoholic. Or refusing to watch a provocative show because you'll end up like one of the characters. Relax. Dressing up as Cruella De Vil doesn't make you hungry for dog.

Think of structured power playing as a journey to variety, a way of expanding your sexual palette. Discovering something you like in bed doesn't turn you into something less than or different from, it turns you into something more—everything you are, plus this new thing. In the human mosaic everything is a thread that contributes to the creation and growth of who you are. Adding or subtracting a single thread doesn't change the pattern.

The Painfully Obvious Conclusion

Sexual power playing depends on having a partner who'll be there for you physically and emotionally. Trust and lust sit side by side like a pair of shears, joined so that they cannot be separated even though they often move in opposite directions.

If you're willing to give it a go, sexual power playing can lead to ever greater levels of intimacy with your partner and place more space between concerns about your body and your ability and willingness to enjoy sex. Thoughts that your thighs might be bigger than you'd like tend to pale when your body experiences the dawn of new horizons.

Keeping Yourself
Safe for Sex

You're not the only one worrying the stars off the flag. Your partner is, too. He's worried that your relationship is in a tailspin it may never recover from and that he's powerless to stop it. That's why there's a whole chapter written for him—how he can make you feel less vulnerable, more desirable, and deeply loved. The chapter also shows him how to avoid bonehead maneuvers that make things worse. You know, like buying you lingerie two sizes too big.

You also need some strategies on the careless comment or cruel insult. Some men make honest mistakes and say what they didn't mean. Other men are so cruel it feels like they're using words for stabbing practice. I'll show you how to prevent or manage these hurtful events without sidelining yourself from progress.

13

WHAT TO DO WHEN A FRIEND, A DATE, OR YOUR PARTNER CRITICIZES YOUR LOOKS

"I was teased horribly by boys during middle school because I was a little pudgy and had frizzy hair. Today, I'm not fat at all, but every time I take off my clothes, I feel like that pudgy little girl about to get teased again, only this time by my partner. Once a couple of boys tease you, it feels like they all will, even when they turn into men who know better."

—Melissa, 22, Richmond, Virginia

Once, in the middle of making love, a girlfriend heard her boyfriend say, "You know what would make this even hotter? *If you sucked in your stomach.*"

My girlfriend was devastated. How do you respond to that kind of cruelty? With counter-insults? By ignoring it? By talking it out right then and there or waiting for a better time? And what should you say?

Tactless comments, backhanded compliments, subliminal cheap shots, stealth insults, or intentional slams all have the power to wound you emotionally, especially from guys you're interested in or are in a relationship with. The insults can be overt ("*You'd look a lot prettier if you lost ten pounds."*) or covert (*"Do you think it's a good idea for you to order dessert?"*). It can be private (buying you a push-up bra as a gift) or silent (spending forty-five minutes in the bathroom getting ready only to be greeted with silence when you come out). The list goes on. Before we talk about the best ways to respond to insults, it's worth pointing out something you might not be all that conscious of...

You Are Constantly Being Put Down by Everything around You

From the moment you get up to the minute you lie down, you get slapped by subtle put-downs. Oh look, there's an ad that says you're too fat. Oh, there's a commercial that says you're out of shape. And there's one that says you're looking a little old. Everywhere you go, everywhere you look, everything you read, everything you see on TV is a subtle put-down. If you only had this product or used that service you'd be good enough, hot enough, worthwhile enough. And because you don't, you're not. Your self-esteem is constantly under attack. Your physical appearance is constantly being questioned. Your self-worth is always being pegged to your attractiveness. Once you realize just how many subtle slights and chronic cheap shots you endure during the course of the day, it's easy to see why a careless comment, let alone an abusive insult, from someone you like can feel so devastating.

It's precisely because you're in such an emotionally vulnerable place about your looks that you have to consider the first rule of handling an off-putting remark. And that's to ask yourself...

Is It Really an Insult?

When you are unusually self-conscious, every comment about your appearance can feel like a personal attack. Even when somebody pays you a sincere compliment, you're likely to seize on some aspect of it and make it fit whatever you already feel about yourself. If somebody says, "You look good today," you will seize on the word *today*. Because "today" clearly means you looked like the hindquarters of bad luck yesterday.

When you have a story running through your head, you tend to make everything fit the story. This is especially true for comments that are open to interpretation. There is often a great expanse of territory between what was said and what you heard. Faced with a questionable comment, you should always pause and ask yourself, "*Given that I'm sensitive about my appearance, is this comment something that a body-confident woman would consider an insult?*" Because if the answer is no, then you should let it roll off you like water-repellent fabric.

If It Has Testicles or Tires, You'll Have Trouble

Some comments, like the one from my girlfriend's unbelievably cruel boyfriend, are just flat-out insults—offensive to the core and cutting to the bone. You can tell when something is a legitimate insult by the way grief, hurt, and rage roil in a boiling emotional caldron.

In addition to the normal reaction that most people have to a cutting comment, body-conscious women often have to fight against something bigger than the hurt: believing in the insult. It can feel like a confirmation of all that you believe is awful in you. Like you just got exposed for trying to hide the ugly truth. That's why even a careless, unintended comment sends so many women into a deep depression. Underneath the initial anger, they *agree* with the insult. They accept it as a terrible validation of their worst fears. The first step to formulating an appropriate response is to…

Acknowledge Your Feelings

An insult is bad enough—stuffing your feelings and building up pressure just creates more problems. Do not pretend there's nothing wrong. Your feelings are a key part of your internal guidance system. Pain is a signal that something's wrong. Accept the signals so you can deal with them effectively.

Instead of burying your feelings, notice them. If they could talk, what would they say? Once you sort out your feelings, you're in a better position to recover. When feelings own you, they can wreak havoc. When you own the feelings, you can be an agent for positive change.

The most powerful way to frame your response is to consider the insult as another commercial on TV with a negative message about your value. That insult is no truer of you than the thirty-second spot telling you happiness comes in a size two dress. When a commercial offends your sensibility, you can talk back, change the channel, turn it off, or click the mute button. You have fewer options when a human being does it, but it begins with...

Fighting Fire with Fire

I'm not a fan of out-insulting people, but sometimes a woman's got to do what a woman's gotta do. And sometimes a woman's gotta do somebody in. Once, a guy told a girlfriend her breasts looked better when the lights were turned down. She replied, "*But your penis is too small to see in low lighting.*"

You're not going to solve much by responding to your partner's cutting comment with one of your own, but for some women it's a legitimate way to respond because it takes back their power and gives people a taste of their own medicine.

This is especially true if you're insulted in front of other people. It's natural to feel like they may accept the insult as true and view us in a negative light. Worse, if you don't defend yourself when you're attacked, people might see you as having a lower position in the social hierarchy.

A counter-insult lets the other person know they can't get away with attacking us. It also keeps us from looking like we're lower in the social hierarchy, but it comes with a few problems. A lot, actually. The first is that you raise the antagonism, which makes it harder to resolve things.

Second, and more importantly, you will be giving the insulter exactly what they were hoping for, and thus guarantee more insults in the future. Their goal is to hurt your feelings. If you "bite" with an emotional reaction, you've given them the satisfaction they were seeking and perversely encouraged them to continue doing it. This brings up a central question…

Why on Earth Would People Be So Cruel?

Happy, confident people don't make disparaging comments about your looks. They don't need to. The people who do it have a need for control, to establish dominance, to maintain authority, to cover up their own insecurities, to subvert you, to make themselves superior to you, or to simply lash out because they don't know how to deal with whatever pain they're going through. This is an important concept that can't be glossed over. An insult is hurled out of need. And that need rarely has anything to do with you. If I don't have the need to feel superior, if I'm not trying to get the upper hand over you, or trying to exert more control over you, or trying to make you look bad in front of other people so that I look good in comparison, why on earth would I insult you?

It is this need that you should concentrate on, not on the insult itself. Because once you understand the need, you can understand fully that *the insult has nothing to do with you.* It is simply a way to satisfy the insulter's need. The insult says more about the person saying it than the person hearing it. This is not some kind of feel-good balm to protect your ego. It is almost impossible to emotionally detach from an insult without absorbing this crucial insight. The insult may have been aimed at you, but you are not its purpose. Its purpose is to fulfill a need to make the person feel better by making you feel worse. They want to see you feel worse or they can't feel better. The insult is trying to prod you into reaction so that you can fulfill the need. By responding with similar put-downs, you are playing into that need. Worse, you'll get trapped into a ping-ponging verbal smack down that'll become a race to the bottom. That's why the best way to handle an insult is to...

Refuse Delivery

This concept is best illustrated by the story of a great Zen master. A mean, vindictive man hurled savage insults at him for hours in front of his students. The master stood there motionless and calm. Finally, the man left, exhausted and defeated. The great master's students gathered around. "How could you endure such indignities in silence?" they asked. "Why did you not fight back with words of your own?"

"If someone gives you a gift and you do not receive it," the master replied, *"to whom does the gift belong?"*

You do not have to accept the "gift" of an insult. Counter-insults, as the Zen master brilliantly demonstrated, aren't just an acceptance of an unwelcome gift; they're proof that you signed for the package, opened it up, and hung it on your wall.

The beauty of the Zen master's story is not only that you can decline the "gift," but also that you can avoid stooping to a level that does not serve you. It's a great reminder that spitting at the sky soils your face.

While the Zen master's response to verbal attacks is illuminating, it would be hard for mere mortals to sit in silence as they are insulted. What you need is a standardized response that keeps to the spirit of the Zen master's lesson. It is simply this:

Thank you for your gift, but I think you should keep it.

If they continue down the same path, you can simply repeat the thought in different words: *"That's very generous of you, but I can't accept that either."*

Another way of refusing the "gift" and keeping your dignity is to say, "Thank you for your opinion." It reminds the insulter and witnesses, if there are any, that any opinions expressed are those of the speaker and not necessarily of management. In some ways, this really ends the conversation. What is there left to say?

When It's Your Boyfriend or Husband Making the Insults

As effective as these responses are with strangers, friends, even dates, it isn't feasible or desirable to leave it at that if you're in a serious relationship. If your partner makes a questionable comment or delivers an explicit insult, you need to have a conversation.

When it comes to teasing, men can sometimes fall off the stupid tree and hit every branch on the way down. Teasing is our mother tongue, and sometimes we don't know when we've gone too far. Your partner may not even realize that he's putting you down or know the true effect of his words. If the comment was simply male teasing gone awry, then it's a simple fix—tell him it hurt your feelings. Decent guys will know they've crossed a line and will avoid it in the future.

If the insults are explicit and unmistakable, then you need to have a bigger conversation. This can be problematic in a number of ways, not the least of which is staying calm and on purpose. After all, you were verbally attacked—it's only human to be defensive.

It's natural to avoid difficult conversations because everyone feels uncomfortable, but if you don't deal with it—and quickly—you'll just prolong the agony, build resentment, and blow the situation way out of proportion. This nine-step process for handling difficult conversations will help you manage the situation quickly and avoid a repeat of the offense in the future.

1. Center yourself

Talk when you're calm. Your attitude will have a strong influence on the outcome. Assume the best—that he didn't mean the comment (even if he did). You'll approach the conversation in a better state of mind. If you calmly discuss, rather than emotionally attack, you have a better chance at getting a sincere apology and stop future insults. Check your attitude—if you think it's going to be a difficult conversation, it probably will be. If you believe a lot of good will come out of the conversation, it probably will. Visualize the outcome you're hoping for. The most important part of the conversation is to modulate your emotional energy, to stay in charge of yourself and keep the purpose of the conversation from wandering off the ranch.

A great way to center yourself is to pretend it's a year from now, looking back at the conversation that solved the problem. It makes the conversation less daunting and more hopeful.

2. Get clear on your goal

Is it to simply stop the insults? Make him feel as bad as he made you feel? Or repair the relationship and make it stronger? You can stop the insults by throwing a fit, making him feel bad, and letting whatever anger and resentments he has go underground where they'll make an appearance later. But if the goal is to repair the relationship, then you can work as a team with a shared goal. Be clear about what a successful outcome looks like.

3. Focus on the issue, not your partner

Avoid the "Blame Frame," where you frame the situation as a deliberate personal attack. Blaming him for the comment will make him defensive and hostile. Focusing on the hurt you experienced will soften him and keep him open to the possibility that he needs to change his behavior.

4. Thank him for his willingness to talk

Always start and end by thanking him for his willingness to have

an open dialogue. It's a welcoming way to start and a gracious way
to end.

5. Start by asking for his point of view

Open the conversation with something like, "I need your help
processing the comment you made earlier. It would be helpful if I
understood your point of view. Did you mean it in the way that it
came out?" By asking for his point of view, you'll not only defuse
the situation (you're showing a willingness to listen), but you will
also get valuable data to form your next move.

6. Be okay with being wrong

Be open to the possibility that you overreacted. This is where avoiding the "blame frame" helps. By keeping the focus on the effect of the
comment rather than who delivered it, you can stay on track. It'll also
give you the opportunity to tell him that given your sensitivities, it
may be a good idea to keep any teasing about your looks off the table.

7. Disagree respectfully

What if he accuses you of being unable to take good-natured teasing? You can say, "I think we have different perceptions about the
meaning of the comment, and I'd really appreciate you hearing
me out." Then state your case, emphasizing the consequences of
hearing the comment.

8. Paraphrase each other

Nothing can make you feel more understood than hearing somebody accurately restate your position in their own words. It shows
that you truly understand—though not necessarily agree with—
their position. When he paraphrases you, he'll be listening to himself say how much his words hurt you—a powerful way for him to
understand the depth of your feelings.

9. Work together to solve the problem

Whether you agree with it or not, your partner has a point of view. And it will most likely be that he teases everybody about everything and that you're being too sensitive. Ask him how he thinks you should move forward to avoid you being hurt and him being misunderstood. His answer is going to range from "I promise never to tease you about your looks again" to "The problem would go away if you stopped being so sensitive." Suggest a middle ground—you'll contribute to the solution by working on your sensitivity and he can contribute by thinking carefully about the effects of his teasing.

Putting Down the Put-Downs

Men can be unbelievably cruel and insensitive, sometimes by choice and sometimes by accident. But most guys are fundamentally decent, and when they realize that they've hurt the women they love, they'll straighten up and fly right.

It's helpful to understand that almost all women are hypersensitive to comments about their looks. You are constantly assaulted by the fashion, diet, and exercise industry with insinuations that you're too fat, too short, too old, and too out of shape to have any real value. This can't help but get under your skin and make you easily bruised by unsolicited comments about your appearance. Be aware of this. Have some empathy for yourself and all other women who struggle against the same onslaught of subtle put-downs. The lesson here isn't just in handling insults when they come at you but in making sure you don't absorb the media's penchant for put-downs by aiming them at other women.

It is particularly hurtful when a friend, a date, a boyfriend, or a husband insults you. The natural reaction is to hurt back, but the momentary pleasure of revenge comes at a high cost. As the Zen master showed us, you don't fight fire with fire. You fight fire with water.

WHAT YOUR PARTNER CAN DO TO HELP

"My boyfriend flirts with other women right in front of me. He'll compliment a waitress or look a little too long at one of my friends. They're always thinner than I am, which makes me think it's his way of saying I'm too fat."

—Belinda, 29, Cincinnati, Ohio

You may be the one smoking with hurt, but if you have a partner, he's breathing it in. Second-hand suffering is hazardous to his health. He's feeling rejected, hungering for your touch, and having his opinions dismissed ("I love your body but that doesn't seem to mean much to you").

You have shared custody of your body consciousness problem. You may own the issue, but he's making a lot of the payments. He's got a vested interest in helping free you from body consciousness in the bedroom, and my guess is that he'd be more than willing to do whatever he can. So hand him this chapter. He'll get a better understanding of what you're going through and find out ways he can help.

Okay, guys, has she given you the book? Good. Read it when

she isn't around. Otherwise, she'll have one eye on what she's doing and one eye on your reactions. And really, that's not an attractive look.

What about Me?

You're hurt, angry, and rejected. What's especially galling is that nothing on your end has changed. You're still the same guy she was attracted to when you first met. You haven't let yourself go, you're reasonably attentive to her, and other areas of your relationship are in a decent state. In some cases, sex was problematic from the start. In others, it was fine, maybe even great, but then things went south. What happened?

Hearing that she feels too bad about her body to have sex seems ridiculous to you. After all, look at her! She's beautiful! And doesn't she see your hard-on? Does she not know the penis never lies? You start feeling isolated. You wonder how she can sleep so peacefully when you lie there looking at her with so much longing. You resent that she controls the sexual relationship. The sex seems so infrequent and meager you feel like she's doling it out as if she has to make it last until the end of the month.

Thoughts flash through your mind: She no longer finds you attractive, she doesn't love you, you don't sexually satisfy her, she's cheating on you. Sometimes she dismisses your needs as pure horniness, as if all you wanted was a release and didn't care how you got it. She doesn't understand that the only way you feel really connected is when you're touching, holding, and making love. That it makes you feel like a man, a man who knows how to take care of his woman. She doesn't understand that sex—her touch, her warmth, your union with her—is the way you express and receive love. That when sex goes, it's not like a cookie got taken away: it's like the foundation of your love cracked.

Up to now, you've probably been kept in the dark about why

sex dried up like a peach in the back of the fridge. Women don't exactly announce their body anxieties ("Honey, I'm going to avoid sex, and if you guilt me into it, I'm going to shut the lights, wear camouflage clothing, pretend that I like it, hope it goes by quickly, and emotionally detach from it because I feel bad about my body").

Nobody announces their shame. But if you've been paying attention, you've picked up a few clues—constant talk about losing weight, using the gym as punishment, self-deprecating insults, yo-yo dieting, and sometimes purposefully looking bad because she feels there's no point in trying.

It isn't your fault. You are not the cause of the problem, but that doesn't mean you can't contribute to the solution. There are some subtle and not-so-subtle things you can do to neutralize her appearance anxiety and have the kind of sex that will take your relationship to the next level.

Walk a Mile in Her Pumps

Start with empathy. It's probably hard for you to imagine being so ashamed of your body that it would overwhelm your natural desire for sex, but let me paint a picture for you.

Pretend you're hung like a gnat with erectile dysfunction. You're deeply ashamed of it, and no matter how many times your partner says she loves the size of your penis, you know she's lying. You know when you're making love she's fantasizing about somebody who's hung like the Florida panhandle. You know because you've seen the vague look of disappointment when you enter her.

You fall into a mild depression and crawl around in a chronic state of anxiety. You start putting conditions on sex. You avoid positions that give her a full frontal view of your penis. You turn off the lights because darkness makes the shame more bearable. Over time your libido decreases to protect you from the possibility of humiliation. She's frustrated at the lack of sex, but you don't give her an explanation. Shame, fear, and embarrassment stop you from being honest. So you withdraw—even though you love her. You cut back or avoid sex—even though you find her attractive. You reject her advances—even though you hunger for her touch.

And here's the real irony: *You don't have a small penis.* You just think you do. It's objectively average, maybe even a little bit bigger than average. She even tells you this, but you don't believe her. You think she's lying to make you feel better. You know because you watch porn and you don't come anywhere near the size of the guys in those videos. You know because you shower in the locker room, compared yourself to other guys, and came up short. You've checked yourself in the mirror. She's wrong. *The mirror never lies.* You're convinced you have a small penis, and the fact that she disputes it proves how blind she is. She's just trying to make you feel better and you know it.

The point to this story, and there really is one, is that it's actually quite easy to put yourself in your partner's position. And once you *understand* how shame and embarrassment can twist reality into a pretzel, you're empowered to help. Because now you can lay aside any feelings of inadequacy, anger, and resentment. Now you know it's not you she's avoiding, but the potential to be shamed. Now you know it's not you she's rejecting, but her appearance. Now you know it's not you against her, but both of you against the problem.

You mission, should you decide to accept it, is to build up her body confidence, help awaken her sleeping libido, and have the kind of sex that keeps her mind off her body and onto that small dick of yours.

I kid. The first step in your journey is to learn the art of…

Affection for Affection's Sake

It's hard for men to grasp the idea of affection's intrinsic value. To most men, touching and kissing are like riding a train—you get on it because you want to go somewhere, not because the seats are comfortable. It's not some evil plot men hatched against women, it's just the way we're wired:

Touch + Kiss + Hot Woman = Erection.

But women operate under a different kind of math:

Touch + Kiss + Hot Man = Fulfillment Which Might Or Might Not Lead To Sex.

This fulfillment creates a variety of emotional states—feeling valued, appreciated, loved, desirable, essential, protected, important, safe, and taken care of. Those feelings are intrinsically valuable in and of themselves. While it's generally true that women need to feel loved and appreciated to have sex, they resent it when you presume that *every* show of affection has a sexual agenda attached to it.

When a peck on the cheek turns into a tongue in the tonsils, when every hug turns into a grasp of the buttocks, when every massage turns into an eleven-finger rub-down, it doesn't take long before she becomes suspicious of *every* gesture of affection. Now, every time you sit close to her when you're watching TV, she'll scooch away. When you give her a kiss on the lips, she'll give you her cheek. When you put your arm around her, she'll brush it off.

By making affection inseparable from sex, you guarantee a steady stream of rejection. She feels pressured and harassed, and you retreat into anger, resentment, and despondency. Ending the sexual stalemate requires you to understand an essential paradox:

Women don't want sex without affection, but affection doesn't mean they want sex.

I love taking walks through a beautiful park across the street from where I live. I also love tennis. The only way I can get to the tennis courts is to walk through this beautiful park. But just because I enjoy walking in the park doesn't mean I necessarily want to go to the tennis courts. Affection, like walking in the park, is its own reward, and its allure is sometimes ruined if it always leads to the tennis courts. If your partner retreats from you every time you go in for a kiss or a hug, it's a sure bet you've dragged her through the park to get to the tennis courts when she was just hoping to get a little fresh air.

The Art of Agenda-Free Affection

Kiss her and walk away. Put your arm around her shoulders and keep them there. Hug her without going past her belt buckle. Don't grind your hips when you hold her. Show agenda-free affection. Do it for a week and you're going to be amazed at the change in her—and in you. There will be no wiggling away, no turning her cheek, no flipping your arm off her shoulder. The sexual stalemate will recede because without the pressure for sex, she can stop being on guard and enjoy your touch. This is important to you on a number of fronts. It reduces some of the skin hunger that drives sexual desire, leaving you feeling a little more calm, loved, and desired. More importantly, it doesn't just make her more willing to have sex; over time it makes her look forward to it. There's an important distinction between willing and wanting. Would you rather she have sex with you out of obligation or out of desire?

I'm pretty sure you don't want her to "give in" to sex, or count the ceiling tiles as you do your best work. *You want her to want you.* You want her to respond to you in a way that makes you feel like a man—longed for, lusted after, and loved anew. Once you practice affection for the sake of affection, your next step is to…

Create a Safe Space for Her Body Confidence to Grow

Have you ever teased your partner about her appearance? Or made veiled comments about her weight? Or visibly noticed other women in front of her? That's proof that God gave you a brain and a penis but only enough blood to run one at a time. You may have been contributing to the unease with her body by making some breathtakingly insensitive comments. Any comparisons to other women or comments that hint at dissatisfaction with her body will make your chances in the bedroom fall faster than a six-pack through a beer bong. Your job is to make sure that never happens. Here's how:

Don't make jokes about your partner's appearance. This is a hard one for men because teasing has a central place in the way we communicate. It's the driving force of our personalities and the way we show camaraderie. You can't do that with women. Not about their appearance, anyway. Once, a girlfriend came out wearing some new clothes she had just bought. She asked her husband the mother of all relationship-busting questions: *"Do these jeans make me look fat?"* Her husband taught me something valuable that day—that there's a worse answer than yes. It's *"Let me back up so I can take the whole thing in before I answer."* He slept on the couch so long the fabric still has the imprint of his face.

Don't look at magazines featuring gorgeous women and then hit on your partner. My friend Jeff did it once. Here's how his wife reacted: "There is no way you're laying your hands on me after you've looked at all those big-breasted, small-butted women. You're not going to use *my* body to fulfill *your* magazine fantasies!" The only action he got that night was the on/off switch on the cable box.

Don't ask her to do things that invite self-consciousness. This is not the time to switch the stadium lights on and ask her to strip. The same goes for asking her to model panties, swimwear, or doing a modified pole dance. It will ignite her appearance anxiety like a propane torch. This is disappointing, of course, because watching a woman disrobe is a huge turn-on for men, but think of it as a postponement rather than a cancellation. Eventually she will have the confidence to do all these things, just not right now.

Don't pay attention to beautiful women in front of your partner. Shut up and look away. Otherwise it's like telling your partner you wished she was prettier, taller, and thinner. How'd you like it if she elbowed you while you were watching porn and said, "Now *that's* a cock!"

Don't use the wrong porn as an arousal technique. Watching porn together can be an exciting way to spice things up, but the porn you like is probably going to do more harm than good. She's going to compare herself to the women on the screen and feel bad about herself. Worse, she'll think you put the porn on because you're dissatisfied with her body and want to see somebody else's. Instead, let *her* pick the porn videos. That'll ensure a smooth ride for everyone.

Don't buy lingerie unless she's with you. It's like her buying you power tools—nothing good can come from it. Buy her a size too small and she'll think it's a hint to lose weight. Buy her a size too big and she'll think you're calling her fat.

Be specific in your compliments. Saying "I like your legs" is good. Saying "I love the way your legs look in that dress" is better. Saying "It's hard to concentrate at work because I can't stop thinking about how your legs looked in that black skirt" is best.

Show her how you feel about her body. If there's something you like about her body, don't just tell her, show her. If her legs drive you crazy, tell her while you massage them. A touch is more powerful than a verb. A stroke is stronger than an adjective. Compliments have limited effects on body-conscious women because they rarely penetrate the wall of negative judgments. Touch operates on a deeper level because the body can override entrenched thoughts. A pleasurable sensation has more power than a negative thought.

Create an Aura of Complete Sexual Acceptance
The most loving thing you can do for your partner is to make her feel completely accepted, body and soul, without judgment or hesitation. This will give her the confidence that crowds out

apprehensions, leaving a space for sexual desire to grow. The most powerful way to do that is through a series of intimacy exercises that have the power to bring you together in strength, love, and unity.

While these exercises are designed to strengthen the emotional connection with your partner, it may be difficult for one or both of you to sustain the required eye contact, especially when it's done in silence. For centuries, staring into somebody's eyes was considered a trespass into their soul. Read through these exercises, and if you don't feel comfortable doing them, don't. In fact, you have to be *very* comfortable with them because you have to lead the process.

The rewards, however, are substantial—a completely new, deeper experience of each other as lovers. These exercises are all different forms of saying "I truly love and accept you exactly as you are." You don't have to do all of them. Pick the ones you feel most comfortable with and follow the instructions. Don't treat the exercises as a prelude to sex. Be sure to talk to each other about what you experienced. If sex feels like a natural next step, then take it, but only if she initiates it.

The belly button balance

Naked, lie side by side but in opposite directions (head to feet as opposed to head to head if you were sleeping). Put your right hand on each other's bellies, feeling your abdomens rise and fall as you breathe. After a while your breathing patterns will naturally coordinate, furthering the sense of oneness. Most couples report a strong sense of being "aligned" with each other. Do this for about five minutes.

The heart heater

Sit naked with your legs wrapped around each other's waist. Stare into each other's eyes and breathe in unison. Put your right hand on each other's hearts and stay there for a few minutes.

The three points of contact (legs, hands, heart) deepen a sense of unity and connection.

The observatory

Get naked and sit cross-legged, face to face with your partner. Knees touching. Your hands are resting on her knees, palm up. She puts her hands on yours, palms down.

Now, look into each other's eyes. In the first part of this exercise she receives your gaze while you bestow it. Note the color, the size of the pupil, and other features. You'll notice a lot of judgments come up (good and bad). Make mental notes but don't break the silence or the eye contact.

Now take a break and cover your eyes with your hands for about a minute. Then place your hands in the same position as before and stare into each other's eyes. But this time reverse roles. Receive her gaze. Let yourself be looked at. It's a completely different feeling because you're allowing her into you just as she's allowing you into her. As the observer becomes the observed, it might feel like you don't know where you begin and she ends. That's the point—to experience unity. It's not unusual at this point for people to cry as they notice how many barriers they've put up against the partner they love. As those barriers evaporate (remember, you must keep at this in silence for a few minutes), you'll feel vulnerable, exposed, and fragile. And as you realize that you can be all of those things *safely* in front of your partner, your emotional closeness grows.

The star-crossing

Get naked. Hmmm. Why does all my advice start with the words "get naked"? Gotta talk to my shrink about that. Anyway, lie down on a rug and spread your arms wide. Your legs should be about shoulder-width apart. Facing you, your lover stands over your crotch, sits her butt down on the ground between your legs, and mashes her butt cheeks against your crotch. She then lies back and spreads her arms out next to your feet. She puts her hands on your feet and keeps them there. She spreads her legs over yours so that her feet are next to your hands. Hold her feet. If you could see it from above it looks like you've formed a star.

Notice the position. Your genitals are facing hers but not touching. The space between them carries a very interesting vibe. You're sexually vulnerable but emotionally connected (symbolized by the touching of each other's feet).

The exercise brings up different feelings depending on whether your legs are over or under your lover (make sure to take turns). Either way, the point is to experience vulnerability and support simultaneously.

Fingertip trespasso

Sit across from each other, naked, with knees touching. Raise both your hands, with only the smallest part of your fingertips touching (your right hand to her left, your left to her right). Then stare into each other's eyes without saying a word. Concentrate on your partner's left eye, as it seems to heighten the experience.

Harmonious breathing

Naked, sit facing each other with legs wrapped around each other's waists. Look in each other's eyes. Inhale in unison. Breathe at the same tempo, same time, same space. Breath and vision can create union. Look deeply into the left eye of your partner. Then change to the right eye. Now change the breathing pattern. You exhale while your partner inhales. After a couple of minutes reverse. She inhales while you exhale. Now breathe in unison. Put your right hand on her heart. She does same. Feel each other's heartbeat.

Ramping Up for Sex

Let's review. You're showing agenda-free affection, which has brought you physically closer. You've created a shame-free environment by reeling in questionable comments and introducing some manners to your media and porn habits. And with the intimacy-building exercises you've created a deep sense of union and acceptance. She will be far more receptive to sex than she's ever been. Now follow through by...

Being her idea of a good lover, not yours

Now that we've laid the foundations for her libido to grow, it's time for you to seal the deal. If you want sex, better sex, hell, *any* sex, then you're going to have to find ways to light her up like an all-night liquor store. The first step is understanding that women's sexuality is contextual. They need to feel comfortable, safe, and relaxed to have sex, and they usually get in the mood by finding ways to transition from the stress in their lives to their sexuality. Pay attention to the environment and make sure you...

Don't kill the mood you're trying to get her into

You can't get her in the mood with toenail clippings on the nightstand or a pile of shelled pistachios littering the kitchen counter. You can't set a mood when your breath is so bad she can see the words float out of your mouth. You can't set a mood when she's exhausted and she can see dirty dishes in the sink that you could have taken care of. Exhaustion is one of the biggest reasons women decline sex. This was reflected in *The Sex Inspectors* series where every woman we talked to said it was a huge bone of contention. Yet the men in their lives did little to help things out. The problem was so common that we came up with a mantra for the men:

If you want more sex, do more housework.

When the men in our show actually helped around the house, their sex life *immediately* improved. It isn't just that the women had more energy for sex; it's that their resentment at having to carry most of the burden melted away, releasing waves of respect and appreciation for their partners. Don't let the vacuum cleaner cock-block you. Roll it out of the closet so you can roll yourself into the bedroom.

Are you helping or hurting?

There's a pretty simple way of determining whether you're warming the path to sex or blocking it with boulders. Look at yourself and your surroundings and ask, "*Am I setting a mood or killing it?*"

Once you get your self-sabotaging handled, your homework is to find out what turns her on and get good at doing it. If she's read most of this book, she should have done enough self-exploration that she can recite her sexual alphabet by memory. Your job is to get her to communicate it to you. You can help the process with...

The foreplay forum

Lie down in a naked embrace under the covers and take turns asking and answering the following questions:

"*Nothing puts me in the mood more than when you...*"
"*I get really turned on when you...*"
"*I love it when you...*"
"*One thing we haven't done that I'd love to try is....*"

Foreplay forums allow you to exchange sexual ideas in a judgment-free zone. The goal is to create a relaxed setting that melts inhibitions, collects valuable data, and introduces a bit of playfulness.

Ask her for a kissing lesson

Kisses are the keys to her kingdom. If you get that wrong, it doesn't matter what else you can do right because you probably won't get the chance to do it. *Ask her to demonstrate what she considers a sexy kiss.* Be a good student—shut up and do what you're told. Kissing is so important to your ability to light up her libido that it's worth going over a few points:

- Be gentle. Start slow and build to a crescendo.
- Move your tongue smoothly. Think swirl, not darts.
- Vary the pace from passive to active, from slow to fast, from back and forth, from dry to wet, from gentle and wild.
- Breathe through your nose. It prolongs the kiss.
- Create anticipation by going in for a kiss, stopping before your lips meet, holding the moment the way a pianist holds a chord, then resolving it gently.
- Close your eyes. Nothing ruins the romance more than two giant beach balls staring at you.
- Make sounds. Small, almost imperceptible sounds. Communicate what you like and what you're feeling through noises, not words. A tiny rumble here, a soft moan there.
- Kiss your partner's eyes. The heat of your lips on her eyelids will drive her crazy.
- Let your desire show. Look at your partner with a deep, rapacious, insatiable hunger. The way oil company executives do when they see the Alaska wilderness.

Get her out of her head

It's impossible for her to obsess about her body when she's having an orgasm that lifts the house off the foundation. But business-as-usual isn't going to get her to the detonation. Read the chapters on fantasy, talking dirty, and power playing and own the process of making it real for both of you. Don't wait for the cat to bark. *Take the lead. Take control.* You can't expect a woman who's been avoiding sex to lead the process. Make sex an escape from her judgments rather than a reminder of them.

Exercise together

A University of California at Berkeley study provided the first direct evidence that male sweat sexually arouses women. A testosterone derivative in male sweat called androstadienone can elevate women's hormones, create physiological arousal, and change their emotional mood. This isn't a license to smell so bad that she loses her short-term memory. Make sure you're reasonably clean. The research on androstadienone is so compelling that you should...

Let her choose your colognes

Because of its pheromone-like properties, some cologne manufacturers use androstadienone as an additive. Take your partner shopping and have her choose what she likes. Make sure she tests it, as colognes smell differently when the chemicals interact with your skin. And while you're shopping, pick up some high-quality chocolate. It contains phenylethylamine, a neurotransmitter that activates the brain's pleasure center, and caffeine, which can provide a much-needed surge of sexual energy.

Cleaning up your act so you can clean up in the bedroom

Knowledge and wisdom are two different things. Knowledge is knowing a tomato is a fruit; wisdom is not putting it in a fruit salad. Now that you have knowledge of your partner's situation, exercise it with wisdom. Don't contribute to the problem by making comments about her appearance, putting her in situations that exacerbate her anxiety, or comparing her to other women. Contribute to the solution by creating a safe space for her confidence to grow, showing agenda-free affection, and creating an appealing environment for sex. You can't do any of this without taking the initiative, leading the process, and encouraging her to participate. She wants you the way you want her to want you. She just needs a little help in expressing it. Be that help.

MAINTAINING A SEXY FUTURE

How to Keep Everything You Learned from Falling Out of Bed

see a bright, sexy future for you. Most women with low body esteem don't suffer from physical conditions that prevent them from improving their sex lives. That means you're only a few reframes away from a love life that can make the air vibrate with passion. That's the good news. The bad news is that you've been so conditioned to expect instant results ("Lose ten pounds by the end of the week!") that you might get discouraged by the pace of your progress. Don't be. You can't undo in a couple of weeks what took years to build. If I had an instant teleportation machine that would deposit you at the end of your journey, I'd give it to you, but I don't, so we're going to have to rely on taking a trip the old-fashioned way—by putting one foot in front of the other.

The journey begins by understanding a central premise: You don't have to improve your body or your image of it to have a great sex life. Admittedly, this is a difficult concept to grasp because you're surrounded by messages and images that tell you differently. So let me repeat it: *You don't have to improve your body or your image of it to have a great sex life.* I am not saying this to make you feel better or relieve you of the responsibility to be fit and healthy. I am distilling twenty years of research showing that female sexual satisfaction has very little to do with size, shape, or weight. It is not true that losing ten pounds will make sex more satisfying. It is not true that if you got yourself down to a size two, you would liberate yourself from worry and angst. Women who have vibrant, satisfying sex lives can be underweight, normal weight, or overweight. They can be tall or short, apple-shaped or pear-shaped. Sexually satisfied women don't have a particular size or shape, but they do have certain traits in common:

1. They have a strong sense of well-being. The nexus between their health, vitality, relationships, work life, and self-purpose creates the environment for their love lives to flourish.
2. They are sexually competent, capable of bringing enormous pleasure to their partners. They value themselves for what they can do, not just for how they look.
3. If they have a positive body image, it's in great part because they've had and continue to have positive sexual experiences (good sex contributes to strong body image).
4. If they have a negative body image, they still have great love lives because of what researchers call "habituation," the process of getting so used to a stimulus (obsessive negative judgments) that it no longer elicits a response (the compulsion to avoid, hide, or not enjoy sex).

I'd like you to pay particular attention to the third and fourth categories. Some women who have great sex lives have strong body images and some don't. This points to a fundamental premise that you need to constantly remind yourself of:

Liking how you look is preferable but not necessary to enjoying sex.

Quit being so impressed by how much you dislike your body. You don't need to like it to have a vibrant sex life. You need to be sexually competent, have a strong sense of well-being, rack up the kind of sexual experiences that create body confidence, and value yourself for more than your appearance.

Weighty Thoughts

A girlfriend once said something so profound it actually inspired part of this book: "*I am only ten pounds away from having great sex. And I always will be.*" In that one statement she revealed an eternal truth borne out by academic research—you will never lose enough weight to fully enjoy intimacy. When you come from a place of self-loathing, losing weight simply means there's less of you to hate. Diet and exercise rarely improve body image. Thinner women are not more satisfied with their body than normal-weight women. The closer you get to the counter-intuitive truth revealed by twenty years of research, the more comfortable you will become with your body:

Being thinner does not make women happier.

You face a daily bombardment of messages promising love and happiness if you'd just get thinner and prettier. It's easy to fall into the trap of thinking that your love life will improve if you just worked hard enough on your appearance. In fact, believing in those messages is the most likely reason you will fail in moving yourself out of the vicious cycle of appearance anxiety into the virtuous circle of fulfilling sex. That's why it's critical for you to use the research in this book to keep you grounded and on purpose. The road to sexual self-assurance doesn't have to be long and winding, but it does require you to pay attention to the map. By being familiar with the signs, symbols, and scales in this book, you will never wander off the trail by more than a couple of miles. Let's go over some important concepts so that you always know how to find "True North."

Looking the Part

- The majority of models and actresses glorified by the media fit the BMI criteria for eating disorders. They are so thin they most likely have terrible sex lives, given that below-normal-weight women are prone to disease and sexual dysfunction. Get in the habit of admiring beautiful, *healthy* women, and your body image will vastly improve.
- You cannot see yourself as you really are. If you could perceive yourself accurately, your body image would improve. You can get a reasonable approximation of your size and shape by subtracting 25 percent from what you perceive in the mirror.
- Believing that you cannot enjoy sex without first losing weight stems from a foundational belief that you must earn the right to love or be loved. You do not believe that about anybody but yourself. Sex is not the reward for losing weight; it's the reward for being human.
- If you want to immediately improve your body image, cancel your subscriptions to women's magazines. There is a direct cause-and-effect link between exposure to women's magazines and low body esteem.
- The media rarely present the type of women men are actually attracted to. They present women who can make you feel bad enough that you'll buy the products and services they're selling. Companies cannot sell beauty enhancements, diet plans, or exercise regimens to women who are satisfied with their appearance; therefore, they must create dissatisfaction.

What Men Want

Getting male attention is a driving force in women's lives. It's natural to behave, dress, look, and act in ways that capture a guy's imagination. But if you're going to do that, at least understand what men want. Remember...

- Women consistently overestimate how thin men want them to be. This causes an enormous amount of unnecessary pain as they try to attain a figure that men do not consider ideal.
- Men are not attracted to the ideal of beauty presented by most media. Men prefer normal-weight women. Yes, they like women on the thin side, but the thin side of *normal weight.*
- Your partner isn't lying when he says you turn him on. Do not ever doubt the sincerity of an erect penis.

Obey Your Body

Sexually self-conscious women have a hard time staying present during lovemaking and focusing on the pleasures of their body. It's important for you to become more sensitive about what your body needs, provide it, and enjoy it. A couple of important things to keep in mind:

- Cultivating sensuality outside the bedroom is an important aspect to restoring your sex life because it trains your body to expect, appreciate, and flourish from stimulating its senses. It will help you pay more attention to what you're feeling than what you're thinking—a crucial aspect to enjoying intimacy.
- Cultivating sensuality means training yourself to ask three questions no matter where you are or what you're doing: *How can I get more physical pleasure out of what I'm doing? How can I make my body feel better? How can I enhance the physical sensations I'm experiencing?*

- Women with low body esteem tend to experience a greater disconnect between the physical signs of arousal (rapid heartbeat, muscle tension, etc.) and a subjective experience of it ("I'm turned on"). Forge a stronger connection by "charting your erotic cartography" and experimenting with different aspects of self-pleasuring.

Libidinal Lessons

Body-conscious women are much likelier to suffer from low libido and low sensation. It is easier to overcome sexual self-consciousness if you have a strong libido, but if you don't, there are ways of bringing it forth:

- Your loss of libido is most likely a subconscious coping strategy your mind uses to protect you from experiencing shame in the bedroom. Settle the conflict between your conscious desire ("I want to be more sexual") with your subconscious unwillingness ("But he'll leave me if he sees my thighs or my belly") by bringing it to awareness and understanding that sex will not destroy your relationship; it will make it whole.
- Smoking and alcohol are libidinal poisons. If you're serious about reengaging your sex life, you must quit or cut back drastically.
- Desire is a decision. You can't decide to be aroused, but you can decide to do things that lead to arousal. First, don't wait for the mood to strike, strike into the mood—by creating an environment for arousal to flourish. That means identifying your erotic cues (the smell of an aftershave, a husky voice) and consciously responding to them. Don't wait to be flooded with feelings. Act on subtle effects and understated feelings. Have "flicker stage" sex and occasionally initiate even when you don't feel like having sex. Ask yourself the

three questions you learned in cultivating sensuality: *How can I get more physical pleasure out of what I'm doing? How can I make my body feel better? How can I enhance the physical sensations I'm experiencing?*

- Exercise is the single best way of raising your libido. It increases blood flow, which improves sensation, lubrication, arousal, and orgasm intensity. Experiment with the 20/70 workout. Exercise with your partner if possible—his sweat contains androstadienone, a compound lab researchers discovered can elevate women's hormones, create physiological arousal, and change emotional mood.

- Develop erotic cues. Porn is a proven way of elevating libidos and activating women's arousal mechanisms, but it's highly individual. Find out what turns you on and buy, rent, or borrow the films that do it for you. Do the same with erotic literature and photographic books. Own your cues.

- Communicate what you like to your partner so that you look forward to sex. Blaming him for not delivering what you never requested will make it easier for you to avoid intimacy or gradually lose your libido.

Managing Your Mind during Sex

Don't try to stop your obsessive judgments—it's like trying to imprison the rain. Crowd them out instead with new experiences and activities that focus the mind. Positive experiences tend to put the kibosh on internal criticisms. You can also practice the art of separating the thought from the thinker. The Buddha always said that negative, unwanted thoughts and emotions are like clouds. They come. They go. Your job is to acknowledge the presence of the clouds without mistaking yourself as one of them. Periodically remind yourself of the following:

- Women with low body esteem consistently overestimate the size and shape of their body by about 25 percent. If you start getting upset about jiggly thighs or poochy bellies, apply the 25 percent margin of error. You may in fact have a big butt, but it's 25 percent smaller than you believe.
- The way you have sex invites the kind of visual inspection you fear. Being still, quiet, passive, and hiding your features in clothing or darkness are ways of withdrawing from activity. Withdrawing leaves you with nothing to focus on but your body. The secret to managing your mind in bed is to be a vehicle for pleasure rather than an object to be looked at. Be active, talk, engage, exchange. Move so you can stop being a sight to see and be a force to be felt.
- Sexual competence builds body confidence. Women who consider themselves "good in bed" report far less appearance anxiety even when researchers held their weight and body size constant. Be one of these women by learning the oral and penetrative techniques in this book. Get competent and you'll get confident.
- Focus on your partner. The more attention you pay to his body, the less attention you'll pay to yours.
- Quell the panic of being touched in worrisome areas by using the technique inspired by my friend Cynthia. When you're alone, close your eyes and touch the body part you have so much judgment about. Feel the heat from your hands and visualize an amber glow emanating from them to the part of the body you're touching. Say, "I forgive you for not being what I want you to be, and I forgive myself for placing such unrealistic demands on you."
- Practice passion's defining characteristic: building and resolving anticipation. Movement creates energy that makes thoughts disappear.

- Be verbal in bed. Talking is a way of participating, and participation gives your obsessive mind something else to focus on other than your appearance. Talking sexy can be as innocent as complimenting your partner's body to as raunchy as telling him what you want him to do with the rocket in his pocket. It doesn't matter what you say but *that* you say. Talking helps you stay in the moment, which keeps you from staying in your judgments.
- Fantasize your way out of appearance anxiety. Cultivate your imagination. Inhabit new people, transport yourself to unfamiliar situations, make love to men you've never met. Take a trip and never leave the farm.
- Play with power. Go light or go *Fifty Shades of Grey*, but go. Acting on your dominant or submissive proclivities is a powerful way to focus the mind on the present.

Good to the Last Thought

An old man was wondering if his wife had a hearing problem. So one night, he stood behind her while she was sitting in her lounge chair. He spoke softly to her, *"Honey, can you hear me?"*

There was no response.

He moved a little closer and said again, *"Honey, can you hear me?"*

Still no response.

Finally he moved right behind her and said, *"Honey, can you hear me?"*

She replied, *"For the third time, yes!"*

I know I'm saying this for the third time, but I want to make sure that you can hear me: sex is not the reward for losing weight; it's the reward for being human. The moment you decide that weight is more important than wholeness you will have forsaken yourself. You are worth more than your weight. Do not forsake yourself. Can you hear me?

BIBLIOGRAPHY

Ackard, Diann, Ann Kearney-Cooke, and Carol Peterson. "Effect of Body Image and Self-Image on Women's Sexual Behaviors." International Journal of Eating Disorders 28, no. 4 (2000): 422–9.

Adams-Curtis, Leah, Gordon Forbes, Peter Jaberg, and Brooke Rade. "Body Dissatisfaction in Women and Men: The Role of Gender-Typing and Self-Esteem." Sex Roles 44, no. 7/8 (2001).

Anders, Sari, and Katherine Goldey. "Hormones and Behavior." Hormones and Behavior (2011): 754–64.

Appleyard, Diana. "Not tonight, dear, I'm feeling too fat: Why half of women say weight worries are affecting their libidos." Daily Mail Online. Published March 30, 2011. Accessed December 5, 2011. <www.dailymail.co.uk/femail/article-1371362/sex-drive-half-women-say-weight-worries-affect-libido.html>.

Armatas, Christine, Wayne Maschette, and Rob Sands. "Measurement of Body Image Satisfaction Using Computer Manipulation of a Digital Image." Journal of Psychology (2004): 325–37.

Arnold, Rebecca. Fashion, Desire, and Anxiety: Image and Morality in the Twentieth Century. I. B. Taurus & Co. (2001).

Aubrey, Jennifer. "Surprisingly, Female Models Have Negative Effect On Men." *Science Daily*. Published November 7, 2008. Accessed November 17, 2011. <www.sciencedaily.com/releases/2008/11/081106122301.htm>.

Baird, Amy and Frederick Grieve. "Exposure to Male Models in Advertisements Leads to a Decrease in Men's Body Satisfaction." *North American Journal of Psychology* 8 (2006): 115–22.

Ball, Geoff, Michelle Doll, and Noreen Willows. "Rating of Figures Used for Body Image Assessment Varies Depending on the Method of Figure Presentation." *Wiley Periodicals, Inc.* 2003.

Baltaci, Gul, Omer Bayrak, Omer Keratas, and Ilerisoy Zeynep. "The Evaluation of Clitoral Blood Flow and Sexual Function in Elite Female Athletes." *Journal of Sexual Medicine* (2009):1185–9.

Betz, Nancy, Laurie Mintz, and Gena Speakmon. "Gender Differences in the Accuracy of Self-Reported Weight." *Sex Roles*, Volume 30. 1994:543-52.

Boisseau, Nathalie, Veronique Diaz, Carina Enea, and Marie Fargeas-Gluck. "Circulating Androgens in Women: Exercise-Induced Changes." *Sports Medicine* 41 (2011), 1–15.

Bradford, Andrea, Cindy Meston, and Brooke Seal. "The Association Between Body Esteem and Sexual Desire Among College Women." *Archive of Sexual Behavior* (2009).

Byers, Sandra and Angela Weaver. "The Relationships among Body Image, Body Mass Index, Exercise, and Sexual Functioning in Heterosexual Women." *Psychology of Women Quarterly* 30 (2006): 333–9.

Carey, Molly, Patricia Koch, Kernoff Mansfield, and Debra Thurau. "'Feeling Frumpy': The Relationships Between Body Image and Sexual Response Changes in Midlife Women." *The Journal of Sex Research* (2005): 215–23.

Cash, Thomas, Cheryl Maikkula, and Yuko Yamamiya. "'Baring the Body in the Bedroom': Body Image, Sexual Self-Schemas, and

Sexual Functioning among College Women and Men." *Electronic Journal of Human Sexuality,* 7. Published June 29, 2004. Accessed December 5, 2011. <www.ejhs.org/volume7/bodyimage.html>.

Cash, Thomas, Kevin Thompson, and Yuko Yamamiya. "Sexual Experiences among College Women: The Differential Effects of General versus Contextual Body Images on Sexuality." *Springer Science + Business Media, Inc.* 2006.

Cassiday, Patricia, Lee Jackson, Sue Lamb, and Doris Priest. "Body Figure Preferences of Men and Women: A Comparison of Two Generations." *Sex Roles* 28 (1993): 345–58.

Choate, Laura. "Toward a Theoretical Model of Women's Body Image Resilience." *Journal of Counseling & Development* 83 (2005): 320–30.

Coren, Apicella, Frank Marlowe, and Dorian Reed. "Men's preference for women's profile waist-to-hip ratio in two societies." *Evolution and Human Behavior* 26 (2005): 458–68.

Cornelissen, Piers, and Martin Tovee. "Female and male perceptions of female physical attractiveness in front-view and profile." *British Journal of Psychology.* 2001: 391–402.

Davison, Tanya, and Marita McCabe. "Relationships Between Men's and Women's Body Image and Their Psychological, Social, and Sexual Functioning." *Sex Roles* 52 (2005): 463–75.

Dixson, Alan, Barnaby Dixson, Gina Grimshaw, and Wayne Linklater. "Eye Tracking of Men's Preferences for Female Breast Size and Areola Pigmentation." *Archive of Sexual Behavior* (2011).

Dove, Natalie, and Michael Wiederman. "Cognitive Distraction and Women's Sexual Functioning." *Journal of Sex & Marital Therapy* (2000).

"Eating Disorders and Media Influence—Body Image from Anorexia Celebrities to Athletes." *Media Influence.* July 19, 2012. <www.raderprograms.com/causes-statistics/media-eating-disorders.html>.

Faith, Myles, and Mitchell Schare. "The Role of Body Image in Sexually Avoidant Behavior." *Archives of Sexual Behavior* 22, no. 4 (1993).

Fallon, April, and Paul Rozin. "Sex differences in perceptions of desirable body shape." *Journal of Abnormal Psychology* 94 (1985): 102–5. Accessed December 15, 2011. <www.web.ebscohost. com/ehost/deliver?sid=1dc8b131>.

Fogle, Emily, Lisa Hamilton, and Cindy Meston. "The Roles of Testosterone and Alpha-Amylase in Exercise-Induced Sexual Arousal in Women." *Journal of Sexual Medicine* (2008): 845–53.

Frederick, David, Negin Ghavani, Maisel Lever, Janet Natalya, Anne Peplau, and Curtis Yee. "Body Image Satisfaction in Heterosexual, Gay, and Lesbian Adults." *Archive of Sexual Behavior* (2009): 713–25.

Gardner, Lisa, Rick Gardner, and Leah Jappe. "Development and Validation of a New Figural Drawing Scale for Body-Image Assessment: The BIAS-BD." *Journal of Clinical Psychology* 15 (2009).

Garner, David. "The 1997 Body Image Survey results." *Psychology Today* 30, no. 1 (1997). Accessed December 9, 2011.

Gimlin, Debra. "Body Work: Beauty and Self-Image in American Culture." *Feminist Formations* 15 (2003).

Gorzalka, Boris, and Cindy Meston. "Differential Effects of Sympathetic Activation on Sexual Arousal in Sexually Dysfunctional and Functional Women." *Journal of Abnormal Psychology* 105, no. 4 (1996): 582–91.

———. "The effects of immediate, delayed, and residual sympathetic action on sexual arousal in women." *Behaviour Research and Therapy* 34 (1996): 143–8.

———, and Paul Trapnell. "Spectatoring and the Relationship Between Body Image and Sexual Experience: Self-Focus or Self-Valence?" *Journal of Sex Research* (1997).

Hoyt, Wendy, and Lori Kogan. "Satisfaction with Body Image and Peer Relationships for Males and Females in a College Environment." *Sex Roles* 45 (2001): 199–215.

Hume, Deborah, and Robert Montgomerie. "Facial attractiveness signals different aspects of 'quality' in women and men." *Evolution and Human Behavior* 22 (2001): 93–112.

Hurst, Shannon, and Michael Wiederman. "Body size, physical attractiveness, and body image among young adult women: Relationships to sexual experience and sexual esteem." *The Journal of Sex Research* 35 (1998): 272–81.

Kiefer, Amy, and Diane Sanchez. "Body Concerns In and Out of the Bedroom: Implications for Sexual Pleasure and Problems" *Archive of Sexual Behavior* 36 (2007): 808–20.

Ma, Yanlei, and Huanlong Qin. "Pelvic floor muscle exercises may improve female sexual function." *Medical Hypotheses* 72 (2009).

Mahar, Matthew, Suzanne McDonald, Thomas Raedeke, and David Rowe. "Multitrait–Multimethod Investigation of a Novel Body Image Measurement Technique." *Research Quarterly for Exercise and Sport* (2005): 407–15.

Marika, Tiggeman, and Amy Steer. "The Role of Self-Objectification in Women's Sexual Functioning." *Journal of Social and Clinical Psychology* 27, no. 3 (2008): 205–25.

Meston, Cindy. "Sympathetic Nervous System Activity and Female Sexual Arousal." Department of Psychology, University of Texas at Austin, Texas (2000).

Miller, Erica, Jane Smith, and David Trembath. "The 'Skinny' on Body Size Requests in Personal Ads." *Sex Roles* 43 (2000):129–41.

Nobre, Pedro, and Jose Pinto-Gouveia. "Differences in Automatic Thoughts Presented During Sexual Activity Between Sexually Functional and Dysfunctional Men and Women." *Springer Science + Business Media*, LLC (2007).

————. "Dysfunctional Sexual Beliefs as Vulnerability Factors for Sexual Dysfunction." *Journal of Sex Research* (2006): 68–75.

Sabini, John, and Jason Weeden. "Physical Attractiveness and Health in Western Societies: A Review." *American Psychological Association* (2005).

————. "Subjective and Objective Measures of Attractiveness and Their Relation to Sexual Behavior and Sexual Attitudes in University Students." *Archive of Sexual Behavior* (2007).

Shields, Vickie Rutledge, and Dawn Heinecken. *Measuring Up: How Advertising Affects Self-Image.* University of Pennsylvania Press, 2002.

Singh, Devendra. "Adaptive Significance of Female Physical Attractiveness: Role of Waist-to-Hip Ratio." *Journal of Personality and Social Psychology* 65(2) (1993): 293-307.

Tantleff-Dunn, Stacey, and J. Kevin Thompson. "Romantic Partners and Body Image Disturbance: Further Evidence for the Role of Perceived-Actual Disparities." *Sex Roles* 33 (1995).

Townsend, John, and Timothy Wasserman. "The Perception of Sexual Attractiveness: Sex Differences in Variability." *Archives of Sexual Behavior* 26, no. 3 (1997): 243–68.

Wiederman, Michael. "Women's body image self-consciousness during physical intimacy with a partner." *Journal of Sex Research* 37 (2000): 60–68.

ACKNOWLEDGMENTS

This book never would have seen the light of day if it hadn't been for my sister, Vicky Alvear Shecter, who kept me focused with a blend of wisdom, encouragement, and the occasional threat. At times it felt like she believed in this book more than I did.

I'd also like to thank Lisa McLeod, who convinced me that this wasn't just a book, but perhaps the single greatest personal contribution I could make to ease the suffering so many women have about their bodies. And finally, I'd like to thank my agent, Courtney Miller-Callihan, and my editor, Shana Drehs. Both had the option to pass on the book, and they didn't.

ABOUT THE AUTHOR

Michael Alvear cohosted HBO's *Sex Inspectors*, the first sex makeover series on television. He is the author of *Sex Inspectors Master Class: How to Have an Amazing Sex Life* (based on the TV series) and *Men Are Pigs but We Love Bacon*, a "best of" collection of his nationally syndicated sex advice column *Need Wood? Tips for Getting Timber*. He's been a frequent contributor to National Public Radio's "All Things Considered," and his culture critiques have appeared in *Newsweek*, *Washington Post*, *Reader's Digest*, *New York Times*, *Los Angeles Times*, and numerous other dailies.

Josh Hobgood Photography